City at the
Crossroads

The Pandemic, Protests, and Public Service in Albuquerque

By Joline Gutierrez Krueger

First Edition published 2022 by the City of Albuquerque Arts & Culture Department
Printed by LightningSource/IngramSpark.
Publication of this book is made possible through a collaboration with the
One Albuquerque Fund, with proceeds from the book being donated to the fund.
Library of Congress Cataloging-in-Publication Data TK
Library of Congress Preassigned Control Number 2021923001
Krueger, Joline Gutierrez, 1957-
City at the Crossroads: Joline Gutierrez Krueger
Includes appendices and index.
978-1-7371976-0-7
        1.   HISTORY / United States / State & Local / Southwest (AZ, NM, OK, TX)
Designed by Robin Hesse

Cover art by Kate Coucke

To my sons, who never complained about having a mother glued to her laptop at all hours of the day, night, and weekends; and to all of those whose lives have been forever changed or lost to COVID-19 and the violence of our times.

TABLE OF CONTENTS

The Keller family dons masks, one of the symbols of the pandemic. Photo courtesy Mayor's Office, City of Albuquerque.

The Essential and Entangled Nature of Stories and Service

by Elizabeth J. Kistin Keller, First Lady of Albuquerque
January 2022, Albuquerque, New Mexico

In the fall of 2020, we were putting our daughter, Maya, to bed after what felt like a particularly exhausting day for everyone, and I said, "You know what kiddo?! I am so proud of you. You know neither daddy nor I ever did second grade in a pandemic." She stopped what she was doing and looked back at me. "Really?" she asked, "But did you do kindergarten or fifth grade in one?" While we've joked since that this may have been her subtle way of asking just how old Tim and I were back in 1918, I believe her question also reflected a familiarity with the kind of resilience she was seeing from her teachers, from her family, and from the wider Albuquerque community. It reflected her sense that we are a community that knows how to do hard things, that knows how to adapt, and that knows how to take care of each other.

Key to Albuquerque's resilience, we've realized, are our stories and our service. When COVID-19 hit home in March 2020, we found ourselves—as families and as a city—in an era of unprecedented uncertainty, an era where there were no easy answers, only hard decisions. As we grappled with the twin pandemics of COVID-19 and systemic racism, our schedules, roles, and routines shifted rapidly. After bedtime with the kids, Tim and I would catch up on the day, return work calls and emails, and pour over stories that educated and guided and inspired us, stories that shaped the hard decisions the leadership team at the City was making every day. We listened and learned from stories of past and present pandemic responses and stories about what our future might be; stories in books and articles, and stories in text messages, voicemails, and video clips; stories from around the nation and across the globe and stories from families and communities here at home; stories of grief, anger, exhaustion, fear, hope, pride, optimism, and love; stories of where the team made big impacts and stories of where and how we fell short.

Together, these stories shaped the services the City of Albuquerque and community partners have mobilized and adapted over and over again to meet evolving needs. Stories from our community influenced the hundreds of thousands of meals city workers delivered to seniors and the multiple ways neighbors stepped up to buy groceries and share critical supplies as well. Stories enabled city government to tailor wellness hotels for families experiencing homelessness and the childcare provided for essential workers at community centers across town.

And the many stories of service, strength, and resilience inspired others to engage, as well. First responders came in between shifts to donate

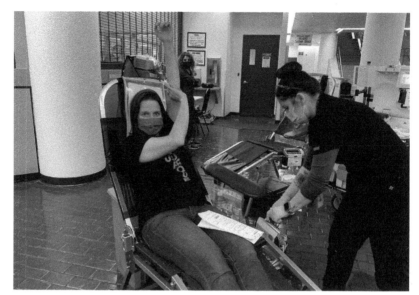

First Lady Keller gives blood during the pandemic. Photo courtesy Mayor's Office, City of Albuquerque.

Brewers and distilleries made hand sanitizer, which was in shortage at the beginning of the pandemic. An employee of Cantero Brewing (now Lizard Tail Brewing) donated hand sanitizer they'd manufactured. Photo courtesy Mayor's Office, City of Albuquerque.

First Lady Liz Keller and Mayor Tim Keller at the Albuquerque International SunPort runway to greet First Lady Dr. Jill Biden. Photo courtesy Mayor's Office, City of Albuquerque.

blood and public servants cancelled Valentine's Day plans to instead pour their hearts into setting up and staffing emergency shelters around town. Volunteers stepped up to pack food, sew masks, and assist with testing sites. Local distilleries made hand sanitizer, textile manufacturers made masks, and business associations helped distribute free PPE to stores and restaurants to help protect frontline workers and customers alike. As these stories spread, individuals and organizations navigating challenges of their own were quick to ask "What can I do? How can I help?"

As we continue this journey together we are reminded of the essential and entangled nature of stories and service and are so grateful that Joline has captured some of our community stories here. May these stories and others inform and inspire the work to come. May these stories and others, defined by Albuquerque's remarkable resilience and deep love of place, carry our diverse community through whatever comes our way.

Mayor Keller gets take-out from a local restaurant, Red Rock Deli. Tim's Take-Out became a regular shout-out to local restaurateurs during the pandemic. Photo courtesy Mayor's Office, City of Albuquerque.

INTRODUCTION

City Government in Albuquerque during COVID-19

by Timothy M. Keller, Mayor of Albuquerque
January 2022, Albuquerque, New Mexico

Just a couple of years later, it's hard to put 2020 into perspective. It's one of those "well, where to start …" type answers. For many, even thinking in depth about that year is painful. It's the year a lot of us just wanted to end. Fortunately, this book will offer generations to come an at-the-time chronicle of a dozen or so Albuquerque residents, or Burqueños, during a year that is undeniably one of the hardest our city has faced in its 312-year history. In any crisis, the individuals involved ultimately are the best storytellers, but it takes a visionary creative mind to weave those personal stories into a broader picture of the shared journey of a community. Joline has accomplished just that with this book—a straight-forward, primary-sourced depiction of public service during a pandemic and the protests gripping a country, but also uniquely affecting the Duke City in some of our darkest hours and brightest moments.

During 2020, people would write, email, or ask me in line at the grocery store, "Mayor, how are you doing?" As Mayor, I'm typically feeling about as good, or as bad, as the broader city is feeling. In this job, you can't help but internalize the state of the city, because you hear it speak to you almost every minute of the day. Whether it's individual conversations, social media, newspapers and TV, neighbors or fellow parents picking up kids at an APS school, your soul inevitably gets intermingled with the collective soul of the city. But in 2020, my answer to that question was different. During 2020, I felt more tragedy, more pain, and more anxiety than ever before, but I was also more driven, more focused, and oddly more energized than ever before. 2020 transformed at least a generation in Albuquerque, and it transformed me.

To be clear, like most people, I was physically exhausted pretty much the entire year, falling asleep in my car in the garage on three hours of sleep, consuming four giant caffeinated drinks a day, and downing an evolving mix of over-the-counter cold medicines trying to shake a months-long nasty cold. In the spring, I missed significant portions of my young children's lives, and like everyone, I missed my parents, my siblings, in-laws, and my friends. The summer of protests layered in countless nights of phones ringing, buzzing with text messages, midnight meetings preparing for 6 a.m. internal briefings, and adapting minute-by-minute to avoid the deaths and chaos we were witnessing in other cities. It was a "maxed out" like never before. Then, in the fall, spring just repeated itself again, but this time with more bitterness and public frustration. So why did I feel different?

The year 2020 was a once-in-a-lifetime experience where the confluence of public need intersected with the mayor's position in a way that changed everything about typical mayoral leadership. During 2020, one of the biggest issues of the past few years, the much maligned ART (Albuquerque Rapid Transit) project was all but forgotten. Standard issues like planning and zoning, potholes, climate change, trash pickup, weeds, animal welfare, and dozens of other bread- and-butter city issues were no longer front-of-mind for residents. It was all about the pandemic, public safety, and public health, and then it was all about social justice and racial reckoning with our own history. Hopefully, we will never again see that kind of stark crisis reality again, but in some ways it was extremely clarifying for public leadership.

As a washed up St. Pius X High School quarterback, I often use football analogies with our city leadership team and with the public. In football, there are game plans made in advance, and during the game, the coach calls plays, and sometimes the quarterback calls audibles to different plays. But when you are in the two-minute drill, the final two minutes of a game, all of that is out the window. As quarterback, you call all the shots, no time to plan, no time to huddle, no time to discuss, to set goals, you just bark out the play, trust each other, and snap the ball. In the football arena, there is nothing more exhilarating. Being Mayor of Albuquerque in 2020 was like being quarterback during a two-minute drill, but for the entire year.

I woke up every single day in 2020 with zero doubt as to what to do. There were decisions to make—big ones—to adapt, to be courageous and compassionate, and to truly lead our workforce of nearly six thousand employees and our metro area of nearly 900,000 people. Instead of adhering to the roadmap of strategic planning we did when we first came into office, we knew we had to get into pure crisis management mode. That meant problem solving in real time, getting some things right, some things wrong, and learning as we go. I leaned on every little bit of knowledge I could glean from others, from my past, and from other mayors. Being fully engaged and fully immersed in work I hoped would make a difference and gave me a clear sense of purpose. It was an opportunity to truly help a community, not in a typical elected official way, but in our time of need, and that kept my adrenaline going for months. Regardless of how it went, or how it will be remembered, 2020 was a year I was rabidly determined, laser focused, and doggedly empowered to spend every hour of my day, every ounce of my energy, my every power and talent to carry our city safely through.

During those early months, many partners in the community were equally driven by this thirst to make a real difference for our hometown in times of crisis. One of our true partners was Michelle Lujan Grisham, Governor of the State of New Mexico. When she was elected, we pledged to be the first New Mexico governor and Albuquerque mayor that would truly work together. The pandemic was a catalyst for problem solving together for our community. We came to agreement a lot, not always, but in general unifying our city's efforts with the state's orders, rather than falling into divisiveness,

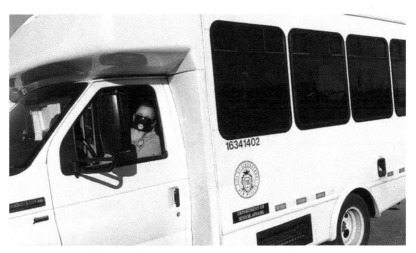
A Department of Senior Affairs employee drives a van for senior during the pandemic, providing valuable free rides.

saved countless lives and livelihoods. We must have talked on the phone almost daily for several months in addition to our teams working through issues at multiple levels. All across America, states had to set health policy, but cities were the epicenter of the pandemic and where the policies either became reality or just a press release.

At the City of Albuquerque, where we provide mostly essential services, and mostly all work in just a few locations, the first question of where should we be became how should we function? How do we continue to operate safely while encouraging people to stay apart? Our administration knew we wanted to preserve jobs in city government so instead of facing furloughs and layoffs, our employees did something amazing that we will never forget—they kept the city running by continuing, and even ramping up, as many of our services as possible, and tackling the public health emergency at hand. We had to figure out how to mobilize community resources so that everyone could stay safe, realizing that not everyone had the luxury to stay home. Fortunately, Albuquerque City Council took, on March 15th, one of the most important and unnoticed acts by amending city government's emergency powers to incorporate public health. This important debate, deftly managed by the city council president, passed on a 6-to-3 vote. This courageous act of sheer political selflessness and unabashed action for what was in the best interest of our community during an emergency, stands out as one of the most critical moments for the city, and by extension the state, in 2020.

Our city's frontline workers didn't miss a beat, and some didn't miss a day of work, despite their increased risks of contracting COVID-19. For some essential workers, like delivery drivers, sanitation workers, and healthcare workers, their workloads increased exponentially during the pandemic.

The executive team that served in 2020 (Lawrence Rael, Sarita Nair, Mike Puelle, Sanjay Bhakta and Justine Freeman) with Electric Playground representatives. Photo courtesy Mayor's Office, City of Albuquerque.

Unlike many other city, county, and even state governments, all of the City of Albuquerque directors got together early on in the pandemic and decided to do everything possible not to shut down. The administration sought to strengthen the safety net the city provides, rather than cut holes in it, even if city employees had to change roles or workspaces.

So everyone shifted. Lifeguards and swim coaches handed out PPE. Librarians redeployed to wellness hotels. Community centers provided daycare pods for thousands of kids whose parents were essential workers, even our own children. The City of Albuquerque focused on safely keeping open—or reopening—the public spaces that our residents rely on. Unlike other cities, we kept our zoo, open spaces, libraries, museums, playgrounds, pools, and kids programs open as much as we could under the state public health order. The City of Albuquerque leaned into a continuation of services that focused on complying with public health orders, instead of closing down all together—a decision that would have hung countless families out to dry.

City hourly workers, who don't get paid or get benefits if they are not working, did construction projects while our streets were empty. Over one hundred city workers acted as inspectors in helping restaurants reopen as health orders changed and new outdoor dining configurations became necessary. City government literally paid small local businesses to not close forever, cutting $10,000 checks to stave off evictions and bankruptcies. Albuquerque approached things differently than many cities did, trying to provide ongoing city services when folks needed it the most. These were all very deliberate decisions made during an emergency, and that continuation of public services saved people's jobs, housing, and maybe even lives.

In addition to service, another way we reacted to and processed the pandemic is through how we have told its story. Early on, the administration had to tell the story of coronavirus to our constituents. Information was changing by the minute, and sharing accurate information in different formats, languages, and with ADA accessibility was more critical than ever. We said, we are here for you, our service to you will go on. We had to tell people—99% of whom had never been through a pandemic before—to stay safe and to stay distant. We had to bust myths that were quickly spreading dangerous, even deadly, misinformation. We had to make sure people knew where to get resources, and who could help. Our message was not simply stay home, because not everyone could stay home.

Our early pandemic public health tenets revolved around ensuring compliance with the State of New Mexico's orders by Albuquerque residents; after all, the city and the state knew that a state public health order is irrelevant if Albuquerque, the largest city in the state, doesn't comply. So when state health orders came down, we took a path of education versus punishment to achieve compliance. We deputized planners, health inspectors, and fire marshals to help businesses keep up with changing occupancy limits, enforced special hours at stores for seniors and people with disabilities, and made sure COVID protocols were followed in high-risk places like nursing homes and the airport. Though there was tremendous pressure to call a curfew in the early days of the pandemic, our city government decided not to implement one, because residents were actually listening to leaders, and we didn't want to criminalize people who were out working a nightshift or caring for a family member.

We were passionate about allowing and encouraging people to get outside as long as they could stay far apart. When many other places were roping off all public spaces, we kept our public outdoor spaces mostly open in Albuquerque. We have many people living in high density apartments, so we had to weigh if people were better off staying in their apartments or playing in hallways, or playing outside, in the sunshine and open air on playgrounds, or in the bosque and the foothills. Many more residents of Albuquerque chose to be outside during the pandemic than any other time in recent past. We transformed twenty community centers into daycare centers for essential workers, taking care of thousands of kids of police, fire, nurses and doctors who had to go to work. We installed WiFi on vans and parked them at schools and in neighborhoods so kids without internet at home could keep learning during virtual school. We worked with the State of New Mexico and Bernalillo County to convert five hotels into homeless shelters and maxed out the Westside Shelter, at times housing 900 individuals and families

An Albuquerque student uses Wi-Fi provided by City of Albuquerque for virtual school during the COVID-19 pandemic. Photo courtesy Mayor's Office, City of Albuquerque.

across the system—and preventing the kind of heartbreaking COVID-19 spikes among the unhoused that so many other cities saw. Then, we felt we had to do our own "New Deal" program to stimulate the economy and keep working families bringing home a paycheck. The result was $300 million worth of investments in infrastructure that the city accelerated out the door to construction companies. In the fall of 2020, looking out my office window became a bizarre pastime. I can see about a third of the city from there, and the streets were empty, with no cars and no traffic. Family pods played in our parks, and construction cranes dotted the skyline, but there were no lights on in any other office building or hotel as far as the eye could see.

During the pandemic, we started measuring positivity rate, number of cases, testing, and vaccinations, and Albuquerque was first- or second-best on nearly every health indicator of the major western U.S. cities. What we have proven over and again is that Albuquerque is a healthier place to live, by connecting to the resilience that has always been here in our community but also in a historical sense, the story of our city and state as a healthful place. From the days of tuberculosis to the time of COVID-19, we've seen that our region is a healthier place to be than other places.

One of the things that changed for Albuquerque during the pandemic was people's realization that we live in a healthy place, where people can have healthy habits and choose to care about others. We have sunshine, fresh air, and room to grow. New residents are now bringing their remote jobs with them and choosing Albuquerque because it's a better place to be. During the pandemic and for the first time in a while, Albuquerque has seen an influx of people moving here to take advantage of our weather, our relatively affordable housing prices, and our proximity to nature. Whether it's kids coming back to go to school at UNM, or extended families reuniting together in New Mexico, Albuquerque has fared better than some of the cities around us as a place to find the quality of life that we learned we needed.

Our city was again compared to other cities in 2020 during that summer of racial reckoning. For the second time that year, cities were the epicenter of a national crisis. At first, the national narrative and frustration spilled onto our streets like so many cities in America, but our city also brought our own unique history into the movement. Albuquerque foreshadowed many of the issues surfaced by the murder of George Floyd. By the time 2020 came, we were already several years into a Department of Justice consent decree specifically because of use of force issues in the Albuquerque Police Department. We had also seen protests during then candidate Donald Trump's visit that led to a reform process of how our city handles freedom of speech and protest. So when 2020 came around, at first we felt we were ahead of the learning curve. We had already done seven of eight on the "eight can't wait" police reform scorecard and had new policies on modern crowd control and freedom of speech protocols. Unfortunately, we were quickly humbled when our own unique 300 years of history with inhabitants of this land since time immemorial collided with the American zeitgeist in a uniquely New Mexican tragedy at the Juan de Oñate statue near the Albuquerque Museum.

After that violence erupted, dozens of community members with vastly diverse perspectives came together for the Race, History, and Healing Project to forge a path forward for the statue and to move towards reconciliation. Later that year, I was able to personally meet with the artists behind both *La Jornada*—Reynaldo "Sonny" Rivera—and the accompanying earthwork *"Numbe Whageh"*—Nora Naranjo Morse. Speaking with Nora and Sonny, and truly listening to several members of the Black Lives Matter (BLM) movement, as well as our own police officers were some of the most profound, transformational conversations in my life, talks that deeply changed and enlightened my own view of what was happening in our city and in our nation. BLM's insight into the national conversation and the Black New Mexican experience was as powerful as Sonny and Nora's Native American and Hispanic perspectives, all deeply infused with echoes of fire fight from hundreds of years ago, embers of which we still feel today in a way that few, if any, American cities could relate to.

With the pandemic waning (temporarily, as we would learn) in the summer of 2020, our city leadership team was perhaps, in hindsight, uniquely flexible, courageous, and ready to take bold steps. In the wake of the Oñate incident, George Floyd's murder, and our own experience with DOJ reform, our city, with city council's help, embarked on what would become the nation's most significant change in the way cities respond to 911 calls and emergency response.

I remember distinctly sitting with the executive team around the triangle-shaped table in the mayor's office at city hall after twenty or so protests. Here I expressed my frustration, understanding that Albuquerque urgently had to find a path forward on police reform, and that the piecemeal suggestions being proposed just weren't cutting it. The Black Lives Matter movement had highlighted so many ways in which our country, but in our case our city, simply was not moving fast enough or boldly enough on the intersection of race and policing. As a nation, we have also been doing a major disservice to police officers by placing nearly every societal challenge on their plates. We were asking officers to solve homelessness, mental health crises, addiction, and poverty—not to mention fighting violent crime.

Sarita Nair, the first woman in history to serve as the City of Albuquerque's Chief Administrative Officer, chimed in with a strong desire to take our most effective pilot programs that we had started over the past couple of years to decriminalize addiction, mental health, homelessness, and poverty and formalize them as a cabinet-level emergency response department. That conversation became the genesis of our nationally innovative Albuquerque Community Safety Department (ACS). It would become the nation's first 24/7, alternative response to non-life threatening 911 emergencies, sending trained professionals and social workers to offer resources that might help someone change their life. ACS frees up police officers to fight violent crime and EMTs to focus on lives in immediate danger, getting people the right help at the right time.

It was another example, following how we dealt with COVID in our own uniquely Albuquerque way, that the Duke City has a remarkable capacity for resilience and innovation. Sometimes it just takes a crisis or two to remind us of how special we are and how powerful we can be. At the end of 2020, our city was a safer place to live in the pandemic and a place where healing and progress can actually happen, even across centuries of deep pain and trauma.

2020 did have a few lighter memories. The absurd toilet paper shortage of April, standing in line outside freezing before Thanksgiving with hundreds of Burqueños just trying to get some Ramen noodles (yes, it's a family favorite), only to get in and find the shelves empty once again. The number of times we all said "you are on mute, can you please unmute?" Playing just two CDs in my car all year (yes I still have a CD player): Sepultura's *Chaos A.D.* and In Flames' *I, the Mask*. Heavy metal fans will understand why.

Fundamentally, 2020 was the year I never had to ask "why?" They say that is the most important question leaders have to answer, and there was never a doubt for 365 days that year. 2020 was a year that I never want to repeat, but it is a year that I have never been more grateful for my family, for the city leadership team, for the frontline workers who kept our city running, and for all of the Burqueños who came together—and stayed apart—when it mattered most. It is the year when serving our city was the honor, the challenge, and the experience of a lifetime.

Downtown Minneapolis (left) and Downtown Albuquerque (right), both images from the summer of 2020. Photo courtesy Mayor's Office, City of Albuquerque.

On March 11, 2020, New Mexico reported its first four cases of COVID-19, including one from Bernalillo County, which encompasses Albuquerque.

1

Sunny Days, Neon Nights

A small but excited crowd gathered January 5, 2020, in the cold twilight on Central Avenue east of Albuquerque's Nob Hill and waited for the magic that they had been promised. Rising thirty-five feet above the onlookers was the iconic neon sign of the De Anza Motor Lodge, which for six decades had been a bright and welcoming sight for weary travelers swinging through the heart of Albuquerque on Central Avenue.

The De Anza Motor Lodge had been a showpiece of modern amenities and Pueblo Indian style when it opened in 1939—a landmark of the old and the new for tourists in search of a good night's sleep and cultural kicks on Route 66. The motor lodge boasted thirty rooms, each with hot water, steam heat, private telephones, and an "air cooling system" for those hot Albuquerque summers. The café floor was speckled with real turquoise and silver. A large curio shop at the center of the lodge sold souvenirs, pottery, and jewelry from Zuni Pueblo, a unique addition brought in by owner C.G. Wallace, a legendary trader with the Zuni Indians, which set the De Anza apart from other motor lodges of the time.

What people remembered, though, was the De Anza's neon sign, tall and triangular and bearing the armless image of the eponymous Spanish conquistador, whose bearded countenance looking wistfully to the north, his striped sleeve tops puffing forth like two beach balls from a green buttoned doublet, the entire bust ringed in neon.

Here on the Mother Road, neon burned brightly from the motels and diners and bars dotting the historic highway, especially along Albuquerque's bustling Central Avenue corridor.

"All the neon that was on the street, it rivaled Las Vegas," gushed Johnny Plath, the third generation of an Albuquerque family of neon sign craftsmen.

De Anza Motor Lodge, Albuquerque Progress, June 1939, photo courtesy Albuquerque Museum Digital Archives, object #PA1983.001.656.

Mayor Keller joined community members to celebrate the completion of the De Anza hotel and apartment complex. Photo courtesy Mayor's Office, City of Albuquerque.

De Anza Motor Lodge Tourist Card, c. 1945, gift of Nancy Tucker, photo courtesy
Albuquerque Museum Digital Archives, object #PA2014.007.049

A Tourist Court on Central Ave, PA Hanna & Hanna February 1938, photo courtesy
Albuquerque Museum Digital Archives, object #PA1980.061.157

"For the brightness, the intensity, the motion, the animation. It was just a wonderful sight to behold."

By the 1980s, travelers had begun to abandon Central and Route 66 for the bigger, faster interstate I-40 that zig-zagged across the country and bypassed Albuquerque's city center altogether. By the late 1990s, motels and businesses on the old route had shut down and the neon lights dimmed, relics of a bygone era.

Once a destination, the De Anza Motor Lodge sat empty, a dilapidated, dreary eyesore. Roofs collapsed. Interiors were ravaged by fire and flooding and vagrants. The grounds were overrun by tumbleweeds, trash, and a colony of feral cats. In 2009, the property was so broken down that its only use was as a film location for a drug deal scene in a *Breaking Bad* episode. The

Street Scene on Central Ave, c. 1950, gift of John Airy, photo courtesy Albuquerque Museum Digital Archives, object #PA1982.180.346

neon conquistador had long gone dark, parts of its metal mooring stolen. But Albuquerque has always been a place of resilience and revival, rising up from the ashes to recreate itself, as the De Anza itself would.

From the earliest days of the Pueblo Indians following the hunting and planting seasons across the middle Rio Grande valley, to the Spanish explorers who forged trade routes and settlements along El Camino Real, to the railroads and the wars and Route 66, each era both imbued and scarred Albuquerque with character and grit and pride, making it imperfect and magical and real.

So it went with the De Anza. After years of neglect and debate over what to do with the property, purchased in 2003 by the City of Albuquerque, construction began in 2017 to transform the crumbling motel into high-end apartments and extended stay units. The plan called for razing much of the property while preserving what had made the De Anza iconic—the rare and rarely seen murals of Zuni Shalako dancers in the lobby basement, the turquoise and silver-flecked floor of the café, and the old neon sign.

Johnny Plath believed no one else should—or could—refurbish the De Anza's sign. Like many of the vintage neon signs along Route 66, it was like a family heirloom, created by craftsmen under the tutelage of J. Wilbur Jones, Johnny Plath's grandfather and a pioneer in the art of neon sign making.

Traffic at Central Ave at First Street, September 10, 1969, photo by Walter MacDonald, courtesy Albuquerque Museum Digital Archives, object #PA1996.006.041

The De Anza Motor Lodge's iconic neon sign, photo courtesy De Anza @ DeAnzaABQ on Facebook.

Jones and his company, Zeon Signs, had been creating signature neon works in Albuquerque since 1938, a year before the De Anza opened.

Jones' son, John Plath, carried on his father's business, starting his own company under the name Southwest Outdoor Electric in 1969 and refinishing many of his father's old signs, including the one in front of the De Anza. When the elder John Plath retired, sons Johnny and Larry Plath took over the business. In 2018, their company took on the restoration of the De Anza sign, a project that took two years.

"All the neon housing was broken, the metal was rusted, paint faded, electrical shot," Larry Plath said. "It was a heck of a job."

Johnny Plath oversaw the crew that removed the sign with a crane and cables, handling the sign as if it was his own child—and his own childhood—which in some ways, it was.

"He was like a gentle grandpa, but one that was often cussing at the wind," De Anza manager David Peters said. "He was so serious and emotional about the work, like he didn't want just anybody messing with his sign."

On that evening in January 2020, the Plaths, other invited guests, and the public gathered at the sign's base and cheered as the light switch was flipped, the neon buzzed back to life, and the magic happened. John Plath, the son of J. Wilbur Jones, the De Anza sign creator, was ninety-one years old and in failing health, but he wasn't about to miss the lighting. His son, Johnny Plath, wasn't about to let him.

"It was their time to shine," Johnny's brother Larry Plath said.

Johnny Plath with a neon roto-sphere he created. Photo courtesy New Mexico Route 66 Association.

Johnny Plath had a grin from ear to ear, David Peters said. It was, he said, the first time he had ever seen Johnny smile.

"He and his dad were just so proud," Peters said.

Two months later, the De Anza officially re-opened its doors with a grand opening. On March 10, 2020, officials gave speeches on the resiliency and history and culture of Albuquerque. City of Albuquerque mayor, Tim Keller, waxed poetic about this city of crossroads—tribal trade routes, El Camino Real, the railroad, and Route 66.

Later that week, Keller took the first steps toward shutting down those crossroads and the city to fend off a new and vicious virus that was traveling like an unwanted tourist across the globe at a terrifyingly rapid and deadly pace. Many in the general public had yet to pay attention to this strange, new virus out of Wuhan, China, alternately called novel coronavirus, nCoV, and COVID-19. Whatever it was called, it was a problem somewhere else, people thought, if they thought of it at all.

Keller and his administration had already begun watching and meeting and preparing for this new plague, whose catastrophic effects or endurance no one could gauge. They had seen the number of COVID-19 cases blowing up in the last two weeks across 114 countries, including the United States. The virus hadn't yet infiltrated New Mexico, but they knew it was only a matter of time. That time of reckoning came one day after the official reopening of the De Anza, with its rejuvenated neon.

Shelley and Johnny Plath. Photo courtesy Shelley Plath.

On March 11, 2020, New Mexico reported its first four cases of COVID-19, including one from Bernalillo County, which encompasses Albuquerque. New Mexico governor, Michelle Lujan Grisham, declared a public health emergency, urging people to avoid public gatherings, sanitize common surfaces, and minimize contact with individuals outside one's household. The World Health Organization characterized the coronavirus outbreak as a pandemic.

The Plath clan's celebrations around the De Anza's rebirth would flicker and fade, just as the old neon sign had. Four weeks later, COVID-19 killed the elder John Plath and infected seven members of his family.

Four weeks after that, the virus killed Johnny Plath, too.

Photo: Minesh Bacrania

After his first ten months as mayor, Tim Keller had garnered an impressive 61% of likely Albuquerque voters who approved of his performance while 16% disapproved, according to a September 2018 Albuquerque Journal *poll.*

2

The Metal Mayor

Tim Keller was everywhere. After becoming the mayor of Albuquerque at the end of 2017, Keller became a ubiquitous presence, favoring daily dispatches of press releases, frequent news conferences, and appearances at every ribbon cutting ceremony, grand opening, march, protest, funeral, sporting event—or heavy metal concert— he could fit into his busy schedule.

Keller, who was a spry thirty-nine years old when he was first elected mayor in a landslide in November 2017, seemed the perfect candidate for the social media age. Young, handsome, and endlessly energetic, he translated well on camera and knew how to use technology to his advantage, posting both professional content and personal family moments with his accomplished wife, Dr. Elizabeth "Liz" Kistin Keller, and their two telegenic children, Maya and Jack, on Twitter, Instagram, YouTube, and not one but two Facebook accounts.

Timothy Keller, 30th Mayor of the City of Albuquerque, photo by Kim Jew, courtesy Mayor's Office, City of Albuquerque.

Keller's fondness for heavy metal music gave him a coolness factor no Albuquerque mayor before him had possessed. That mojo had drawn the attention of the *New York Times*, which featured Keller and his hankering for head banging in Simon Romero's April 2018 article, "For Albuquerque's Headbanger Mayor, Power Comes in Power Chords." The article also earned Keller the nickname "Metal Mayor," for which he had stickers made to pass out to random constituents.

Mayor Keller with members of Anthrax in his office at City Hall, pre-pandemic. Photo courtesy Mayor's Office, City of Albuquerque

Mayor Keller working late in his office at City Hall in 2020. Photo courtesy Mayor's Office, City of Albuquerque

Keller's very decision to run for mayor may have come at a Slayer concert in Las Vegas, Nevada, with older brother Scott, who is equally enamored of the genre.

"We were in the pit, thrashing around, and Tim turns to me and says, 'I'm doing it. I'm going for mayor,'" Scott Keller said in an interview with the *Albuquerque Journal*. "I was an eyewitness to this major moment in his life."

In retrospect, the decision to run for mayor seemed a good one. After his first ten months as mayor, Tim Keller had garnered an impressive 61% of likely Albuquerque voters who approved of his performance while 16% disapproved, according to a September 2018 *Albuquerque Journal* poll.

Some residents, though, were not swayed by Keller's charm. Critics found him all sparkle and no substance, a privileged, publicity-hungry politician with perfect hair and a pollyanna outlook who they claimed believed he could ease Albuquerque's crime, poverty, and homelessness problems with a smile and a slogan.

As a two-term state senator, for example, Keller had fought alongside his constituents to rebrand the troubled Southeast Heights community he represented as "the International District," a far more culturally catchy moniker than the "War Zone" nickname it had earned because of its rampant crime and blight. The new name did little to change the district's problems, but it made some merchants and neighborhood association leaders happy. Keller, ever the optimist, saw such criticism as an opportunity to rally the masses and remind those masses that he was one of them, not some elite schlub hiding out on city hall's eleventh floor, that he knew the hard knocks of the street despite his squeaky clean background as an Eagle Scout, Catholic schoolboy, and Harvard business grad.

So Keller kept smiling, kept showing up everywhere, kept pushing his latest slogan, "One Albuquerque"—his call to unity and action and the name of the foundation created to raise funds to support city priorities, including police recruitment, job training, and outreach for the homeless and the city's youth.

Keller felt good going into the second half of his first mayoral term in January 2020, confident that he had surrounded himself with a good team of people dedicated to turning things around for the city. At the top of his team was Chief Administrative Officer, Sarita Nair, the first woman to hold the CAO position in Albuquerque and an attorney with a planning background who'd served as Keller's chief government accountability officer and general counsel when he was state auditor. Keller's Chief Operations Officer Lawrence Rael was already a familiar face around the eleventh floor of city hall after serving in top positions over the span of three mayoral administrations.

In addition, Keller had selected seasoned, innovative pros, and more women and BIPOC staff to lead the city's offices and departments than previous administrations. Mayor Keller and his staff inherited an economic recession, soaring crime rates, and the embarrassing $133 million-dollar Albuquerque Rapid Transit project (ART), which had ripped up ten miles of

City of Albuquerque Chief Administrative Officer, Sarita Nair and Congresswoman Deb Haaland. Photo courtesy Office of Immigrant Affairs, City of Albuquerque.

Central Avenue and crippled the corridor's small businesses, in exchange for an electric bus system that no one but the previous administration seemed to want. Keller himself called ART "a bit of a lemon." Despite the challenges, by 2020, things were getting better, Mayor Keller believed.

"I felt an energy in the city, an optimism in the city that we were finally waking up from the recession of 2008," he said. "We were booming."

At the state of the city address, on January 11, 2020, before a crowd of about a thousand people at the Albuquerque Convention Center—and broadcast live on Facebook, naturally—Keller ticked off a list of accomplishments: increased tourism, more jobs, more big businesses like Netflix coming in, hosting the largest National Senior Games in the organization's history, penguins at the ABQ BioPark, more youth programs, more solar panels, more LED street lights.

Keller told the crowd that the first steps toward creating a three hundred-person capacity homeless shelter were underway, that by spring Albuquerque's longstanding backlog of more than 3,000 rape kits would be cleared, and that the city was nearing his campaign promise of having 1,000 police officers on Albuquerque streets. Keller was even optimistic that the city could get substantially out from under a Department of Justice consent decree that had handcuffed the Albuquerque Police Department (APD) since his predecessor's term in office over APD's excessive, often deadly use of force from 2009 to 2013.

That was the old APD. Just like the city, the police department was under new management.

"You know, some politicians like to tell you they can change the world overnight," Keller told the crowd at the 2020 state of the city address. "But you might remember I came into this job with some sober optimism, and the last two years have really confirmed this. It's a long road ahead. But to do what

A picture of some of the women who led at the City of Albuquerque during the pandemic, taken for a feature in the Albuquerque Journal.

Shelves at APD full of Sexual Assault Evidence Kits in 2017 compared to empty shelves in 2020, after the Keller administration set out to end the rape kit backlog. Photo courtesy Mayor's Office, City of Albuquerque.

Mayor Tim Keller and CAO Sarita Nair meet with Albuquerque Fire & Rescue Chief Paul Dow to discuss a new fire apparatus for 200 frontline firefighters, August 25, 2020. Photo courtesy Albuquerque Fire & Rescue @abqfire on Twitter

we need to do, to get where we need to go, it's going to take dedication to real change, it's going to take resilience to get through the tough times, and it's going to take courage to see it through."

A week after his 2020 state of the city speech, Keller hit Albuquerque's nightlife with brother Scott, who was visiting from Seal Beach, California. Machine Head, one of the brothers' favorite metal bands, was playing at the El Rey Theater, a gritty downtown venue on Central Avenue just four blocks southwest of city hall but miles and years from the weighty suit-and-tie world Mayor Keller now inhabited. At the El Rey, Mayor Keller could let loose a

State of the City Address at the Albuquerque Convention Center, January 11, 2020, photo by Mood. Photo courtesy Mayor's Office, City of Albuquerque.

little, trade in his tie for a t-shirt, and dive into the dark, sticky throng of sweaty bodies screaming and slamming into each other, lost in the music and the mob, in the smoky, small theater smelling of beer and youth, just as he remembered it.

"We introduced the band together," Keller said. "It was a great night."

After the concert, the Keller brothers posed with the band, throwing up devil horns and feigning tough grimaces, the mayor's clean-cut looks standing out among the leather and tattoos.

"What an honor and a privilege it was to have Albuquerque's mayor, Tim Keller, not only attend last night's show but pit as hard as anyone else in that awesome crowd," the band posted on social media.

"It was the last big fun memory like that before the pandemic hit," Keller said. "The last big concert I got to attend."

Soon, Mayor Keller would be much too busy for anything like that. And soon, anything like that would violate state and city health orders and would be cancelled anyway. Some 7,000 miles away in China, a new and deadly virus continued to sicken and kill. Eight days after Keller's state of the city address, on January 19, 2020, the first confirmed cases of COVID-19 were reported outside Wuhan. The virus would not be contained.

In less than two months after the 2020 state of the city address and the Machine Head concert, COVID-19 would find its way to Albuquerque and blow up Mayor Keller's plans for change. The virus would test his mettle and require the courage of his team and the city itself.

*"I did feel an urgency growing that
this was going to hit and hit hard
and that we needed to be prepared
for it before it did."*
–Alan Packman

3

The Tin Hat Guy

The short article caught his eye. It was late December 2019, and here was something about a novel coronavirus out of Wuhan, China, that had sickened dozens of residents with a pneumonia-like illness. No one had died from it, the article said, and health officials had not determined whether it was easily spread by humans. No one knew how bad it would get.

"Something like that you don't see every day," said Alan Packman, then a member of Mayor Keller's staff.

Most people, had they even bothered to read the article, likely would have discounted any widespread implications of this new pneumonia. It was over there in a city that few people in the U.S. had ever heard of. Alan Packman, though, saw the ominous potential of a virus that could spread far beyond its birthplace—maybe as far away as Albuquerque. Maybe it was worth keeping an eye on. In his Google alerts, Packman added two words: "Wuhan" and "coronavirus." Then he went back to work on more pressing items, including Keller's upcoming state of the city address on January 11, 2020.

"That's a full-time endeavor," Packman said of preparing for the state of the city address. "Double time, really." Whatever that coronavirus was about had to remain in the background.

Packman was playing something of a background role in the Keller administration, an unusual position for a high profile, highly influential, and highly successful campaign manager for progressive Democrats. Packman had managed Keller's campaign for mayor in 2017 and his campaign for state auditor before that. After Keller's mayoral election, Packman served in the relatively obscure position for the City of Albuquerque as Constituent Service Integration Specialist, whatever that meant, though some skeptics questioned just what he was doing at city hall at all.

City of Albuquerque Chief Operating Officer, Lawrence Rael, with storm road crews in 2020. Courtesy of Mayor Keller @MayorKeller on Facebook.

"He took a low-level job in my administration," Mayor Keller explained. "I never met regularly with him."

Packman may have been less in the political limelight, but he still maintained plenty of influence, working with the city's 311 phone system and marketing the mayor's most important projects among his duties. He also kept his ear to the ground just in case he heard any information out there that he thought the mayor should be aware of. Maybe someday that virus out of Wuhan would be important, Packman thought. Or maybe not.

Packman wasn't the only one in Keller's administration who thought COVID-19 might be something worth keeping tabs on. Lawrence Rael, the City of Albuquerque's COO, was having a typical father-daughter chat on the phone with his middle child, Ana, around Christmas 2019 when the conversation turned serious.

"Hey, Dad, have you heard this crazy thing about a coronavirus?" Ana asked. "People up here are really scared about it. This could be something really bad."

Ana, a twenty-one year-old student at Barnard College in New York City and a self-professed news junkie like her father, told Rael that she was troubled that the White House was not paying enough attention to the virus brewing in China. She was worried that the Trump administration was woefully unprepared to handle a serious outbreak should the virus reach the shores of the U.S.—which she believed was inevitable. Ana told her father that she was also nervous about whether the outbreak would grow so big and so bad that it would affect her schooling at Barnard. What happened if the schools closed, she wondered. Ana was concerned about how it could affect her father and his job in city government overseeing the day-to-day operational functions of Albuquerque.

"What's the plan, Dad?" she asked.

Rael smiled at her inquisition. She's very much her father's daughter, he thought. Ana knew where her father's concerns and duties would lie, but he had no answer for her about the plan then. It was still too soon to know, but not by much. Rael made a mental note to bring up the coronavirus matter with Sarita Nair, the city's CAO. Nair, though, was out of commission for much of December 2019.

"I was super sick with pneumonia, or something like it," Nair said. "I was home for two weeks. I didn't see anyone." One of her friends commented, half-jokingly, that maybe she was sick with the new coronavirus.

"That's when I started hearing about COVID-19." Nair said. She had friends in Europe, and they, too, were growing more concerned about the new coronavirus, at least more so than local acquaintances.

On January 25, 2020, the *Albuquerque Journal*, Albuquerque's last remaining daily newspaper, published its first stories on the coronavirus, and then only on A6, the Nation and World page. One of the articles, from the Associated Press, reported that two people in the U.S. had become infected with the new coronavirus—a man in Washington state and a woman in Chicago. Both had recently returned from a trip to China, according to the article. The article also reported that the Centers for Disease Control and Prevention (CDC) expected more Americans to be diagnosed with the newly discovered virus in coming days but stressed that it was still unclear how lethal the virus was or how easily it was transmitted.

"The CDC believes that the immediate risk to the American public is low at this time," the article quoted Dr. Nancy Messonnier, then the most recognizable face of the CDC.

News about the virus, such as it was, was largely overshadowed nationally by continuing coverage of the first impeachment trial of President Donald Trump and locally by the continued brouhaha over Mayor Keller's new and controversial Clean and Green Retail Ordinance, which banned single-use plastic bags at stores. The timing of implementing the ban highlighted the difficult intersection government faced trying to implement policy while suddenly balancing public health worries amid a pandemic that wasn't understood.

Alan Packman was back to tracking the coronavirus after Mayor Keller's state of the city speech was in the rearview mirror. Friends in the healthcare field had started to share their concerns with him about the prospects of a dangerous pandemic and how it would surely strain the medical system. At the end of January 2020, the WHO declared a global emergency after the number of coronavirus infections rose dramatically and continued to spread to more than a dozen countries.

The White House called together a task force to concoct the government's response to the novel coronavirus. Trump imposed a ban on travel from China to the U.S., and then declared that everything was under control.

"Looks like by April, you know, in theory, when it gets a little warmer, it miraculously goes away," Trump assured the crowd during a February 10, 2020, rally in New Hampshire.

Some 2,200 miles away in Albuquerque, Packman was learning that this novel coronavirus—officially named COVID-19 by the WHO on February 11, 2020—wasn't going away. It was coming. Here. And fast.

"I did feel an urgency growing that this was going to hit and hit hard and that we needed to be prepared for it before it did," Packman said.

He asked CAO Sarita Nair for a copy of the city's preparation plan for a medical emergency such as a pandemic. What he received, he said, was more of a distribution plan for vaccines. No vaccine existed for COVID-19 yet, and though he didn't know it then, there wouldn't be a vaccine for nearly a year.

"When I saw the plan that had been sent to me, I knew we weren't ready for what was coming," Packman said. He watched the numbers of cases and deaths rise as COVID-19 took hold in one country, then another. Thailand. South Korea. France. Italy. Iran. Japan. Each country had reported a handful of cases one day and a surge of cases the next. People were dying. One by one, whole towns and regions were locked down. Masks were made mandatory. Hospitals strained under the demand for care for a disease no one knew how to treat. Morgues bloated.

"It was sweeping the globe, and I started realizing that there would almost certainly come a time when we were going to have to keep people in their houses, shut down public places," Packman said. "These are tough choices. But how else could we possibly avoid this?"

It was the unimaginable. COVID-19 began showing up on the front page of the *Albuquerque Journal*, though the first stories were about how the virus was sending the stock markets into a tizzy. On February 25, 2020, the top headline read, "Dow drops 1,000 as virus threatens global economy." It was the worst day for the stock market in two years.

That same day, Dr. Messonnier of the CDC appeared at the White House Coronavirus Task Force press briefing and warned that it was time to start preparing for the likelihood of a major outbreak.

"As we've seen from recent countries with community spread, when it has hit those countries, it has moved quite rapidly. We want to make sure the American public is prepared," the CDC's Messonnier said gravely. "Disruption to everyday life might be severe."

It was time, she said, for governments and businesses to look into telecommuting options for their employees, time for parents to ask their children's schools about possible closures, and time for hospitals to prepare for the worst. It was the last time Dr. Messonnier appeared at a task force press briefing.

Situational Awareness Meeting at the Hispano Chamber of Commerce, February 28, 2020. Photo courtesy Environmental Health Department @CABQEHD on Facebook.

Packman said he knew it was time for him to speak up.

Justine Freeman, then Mayor Keller's Deputy Chief of Staff, said Packman urgently requested a few moments to speak to the executive team, which was meeting on February 25, the same day Messonnier issued her foreboding assessment.

"Alan had never asked to meet with the team before, and I remember sitting at the conference table and Alan being really worried," Freeman said. "That wasn't like him to raise the alarm like that unless it was serious."

Methodically, Packman made his case, delineating a week by week doomsday scenario as COVID-19 inched closer. Freeman recalled that some in the room viewed Packman's admonition with skepticism. Initially, that included Mayor Keller.

"You're a conspiracy theory guy," Keller joked.

"I know, I'm a tinfoil hat guy, but this is going to happen, and we need to be ready," Packman responded.

Keller and most of the team knew that Packman was right. They left the meeting somber but resolved to handle whatever was about to come their way and to protect Albuquerque as best as they could.

"There was a thought that if this was coming we all needed to protect ourselves, go home right away, and stay there," Freeman said, "but that's not what our jobs would allow. We needed to keep working to keep the city safe."

A day later, meanwhile, President Trump continued to downplay the risk of COVID-19 while touting his administration's efforts to slow the spread.

"When you have fifteen people, and the fifteen within a couple of days is going to be down to close to zero, that's a pretty good job we've done," Trump told the nation on February 26, 2020, although that day the CDC reported fifty-eight confirmed cases of COVID-19. The next day, on February 27, with sixty cases being reported, the president famously reiterated his belief that the coronavirus would go away as if by magic.

"One day it's like a miracle," Trump said. "It will disappear."

Nevertheless, Keller reconvened his team February 28, 2020, at the Albuquerque Convention Center for a situational awareness meeting with city department heads, regional government agencies, hospitals, and State of New Mexico Department of Health partners.

"We need to make sure that we have clear protocols in place," Mayor Keller said. "Coordinating efforts is the best way to ensure an effective response if an emergency arises here at home."

In an editorial that ran the same day as the meeting, the *Albuquerque Journal* commended Keller for his efforts to get ahead of the virus but complained that he was holding the meeting in private beyond the eye of the public—and reporters.

"Americans are understandably worried about coronavirus, and they have a right to know what preparations and protocols are in place," the *Journal* editorial opined.

Transparency would come in due time. First, the city had to determine what those preparations and protocols were and what messages needed to be sent to the public most immediately.

"This was a crisis unlike any we'd seen," COO Lawrence Rael said. "It was like a snowstorm you know is coming, so you have to be prepared for it. The clouds were darkening, but this one felt different because we didn't know for sure when it would begin and how long it would last."

One thing was clear: it was time to put into practice the plan Rael's daughter, Ana, had asked about more than two months before at Christmastime. In late February 2020, that plan, though, was still being written.

4

The Disaster Men

There was no hiding it now. Although New Mexico had yet to see its first case of COVID-19 in the early days of March 2020, and the World Health Organization was still a week away from declaring a global pandemic, Albuquerque residents knew something bad was looming on the horizon. And when something bad is coming, panic buying ensues.

With news of coronavirus now reaching the front pages, store shelves were emptied of toilet paper, wet wipes, and bottled water, as if people were stocking up for the apocalypse or a plethoric bout of irritable bowel syndrome. Big bags of pinto beans, a New Mexico staple, and sacks of rice were tough commodities to find. Hand sanitizer, when it was available, was rationed like plywood before a hurricane.

"Due to high demand and to support all customers, we will be limiting the number of sanitization, cold and flu related products to five each per order," a message on Albuquerque's Smith's Grocery website read.

Residents were also buying up face masks, including the N95 respirator masks typically needed only in hospital settings, even though healthcare officials had insisted that for most people, especially healthy ones, masks were not recommended, necessary, or impervious to COVID-19.

News of the impending onslaught of the coronavirus had finally taken hold in the psyches of most American citizens, who watched nervously as cities across Europe began shutting down. A tourist had succumbed to the coronavirus in Paris on Valentine's Day, a particularly stunning death that day in the city of love, where famous sites like the Louvre were now off limits and "la bise," the customary French kissy-kissy cheek-to-cheek way of greeting each other, was discouraged.

Closer to home, the U.S. reported its first known death from COVID-19

Above: Empty aisles at Target after pandemic panic-buying, photo courtesy Andrew Connors, Albuquerque Museum.

At left: Sign at Target on Paseo del Norte in Albuquerque, April 2020, photo courtesy Andrew Connors, Albuquerque Museum.

Roger Ebner, Director, Emergency Operations Department, in front of the Emergency Operations Center. Photo courtesy City of Albuquerque.

on February 29, 2020, in the Seattle area, and new cases were being reported among residents and at least one employee at a LifeCare nursing home in Kirkland, Washington, a suburb east of Seattle. By March 2, the death toll had risen to six. By March 3, nine had died, prompting Seattle Mayor Jenny Durkam to declare a state of emergency.

Roger Ebner saw it all unfold, from China to France to Washington and everywhere in between, and he knew it wouldn't be long before Albuquerque's Mayor Keller would face the same decisions Seattle's Mayor Durkam was forced to make. As the director of the City of Albuquerque's Office of Emergency Management, Ebner had been tasked to help Mayor Keller make those decisions wisely. It was Ebner's job to know where all the fires were burning and to prepare, respond, and recover from those conflagrations.

Each day, Ebner poured over detailed updates from state and federal agencies, including situational awareness briefings from the Federal Emergency Management Agency (FEMA), which tracked everything from weather to wars—and, now, the novel coronavirus.

"We were getting official discussions on COVID since around January 9," Ebner said. "We were entirely aware and in preparation mode."

Even while on vacation in Africa with his wife in late January and early February 2020, Ebner read the daily briefings and kept apprised of what was transpiring across the world and in the city he had tried to keep safe since being hired as Albuquerque's Emergency Management Director in 2013. Ebner doesn't remember the admonition given to the administrative team February 25 by "tinfoil hat guy" Packman, nor does he know the specific information given to Packman about a city preparedness plan, but he rejects the notion that the city couldn't prepare for a pandemic in a relatively short time.

"We are always writing plans, in training, conducting exercises to practice for emergencies," Ebner said, "but we don't want to be the tinfoil hat guy. We want to be reasoned, measured, and motivational."

Emergencies and disasters and how to handle them have been Ebner's vocation for twenty years; Ebner served in similar roles in Montana and Wisconsin.

"I've handled lots of flooding, two airplane crashes, wildland fires, hazardous waste incidents, tornadoes, hail storms, extreme heat, cold weather," he said. "In this line of work, you need to be flexible."

And persuasive. It's one thing to be in the thick of a disaster when all eyes turn to you for guidance and support. It's another thing to plan for a calamity that has yet to happen.

"Our job is to motivate people to prepare for something that may never happen," Ebner said. "It's a job where you have to convince people that trouble might be just around the corner."

Because it always is. Each catastrophe helped prepare emergency management teams for the next one. The confusing, ill-prepared way officials had handled the anthrax scare in 2001, for example, had led to a multitude of changes, chief among them the need for emergency drills and action plans, better equipped health laboratories, better means of communication, and closer working relationships between public health departments, law enforcement, and emergency response agencies.

In 2009, Ebner, then Emergency Management Director for Butte-Silver Bow in Montana, had been tasked with managing the community's response to the H1N1 swine flu, the last pandemic the world had experienced. Many new lessons were learned from H1N1 on how to prepare for, respond to, and recover from a pandemic, and Ebner believed he had learned from them.

H1N1 was the enemy health officials knew, however, a new strain of flu that responded well to old anti-viral treatments. H1N1 was less deadly than COVID-19 appeared to be and older populations had already developed some immunity to it. Within five months of the H1N1 outbreak, a vaccine was available.

COVID-19 was more mysterious. It spread easier, made its victims contagious longer, sometimes without the carrier even realizing that they were sick. So far, COVID-19 was not responding adequately to treatments for flu or pneumonia. There was no vaccine for COVID-19 yet. No one knew how long or how bad the new virus would be. Ebner had a hunch that it would be with the world for quite a while.

"I knew this was going to be a long and winding road ahead of us," he said.

Also gearing up for the long road ahead was Ryan Mast, director of the City of Albuquerque's Environmental Health Department. Like Ebner, disasters of varying kinds made up much of Mast's curriculum vitae.

Indeed, disasters seemed to follow Mast around the country during his career. The Illinois native had just moved to New Orleans to attend graduate school at Tulane University in August 2005 when the costliest, most damaging, and deadliest hurricane in recent U.S. history made landfall off the Louisiana coast, bursting levees, buckling buildings, killing more than 1,800 people, and leaving millions homeless and shattered. That hurricane was Katrina.

In early 2017, Mast had been on the job as Hazard Mitigation Administrator in New Orleans for a few weeks when the only F3 tornado

Ryan Mast, Director Environmental Health Department, celebrates biking during the pandemic. Photo courtesy Environmental Health Department @CABQEHD on Facebook.

ever to make landfall within the city limits blew in with wind speeds between 136 and 165 mph, causing massive destruction in the community.

Then in January 2020, with COVID-19 churning closer to potential pandemic status, Mast began working in Mayor Keller's administration in Albuquerque.

"I wish attracting disaster wasn't the reputation attached to me," Mast said. "That's either bad timing or maybe good for someone in my field."

The coincidences didn't go unnoticed.

"We joked that Ryan had brought the virus with him," Mayor Keller said.

Keller and Mast knew each other from their days as fellows in the W.K. Kellogg Foundation Community Leadership Network from 2014 to 2017.

Mast also knew Roger Ebner, the men having met in 2016 through their work with FEMA. He had nothing but praise for Ebner's steady hand and seasoning as an emergency management leader. Mast was also no stranger to Albuquerque, having visited a friend from his Peace Corps days who had moved here. Albuquerque, he thought, was a good fit for him. Different. Dry. After spending much of his life in wet and muggy climes, Mast appreciated Albuquerque's arid, warm climate and the lack of humidity, hurricanes, and tornadoes.

"It was a nice thing not having to worry so much about floods," Mast said.

The Albuquerque job also offered steadier, saner, family friendlier work hours, an important factor to Mast and his wife, who were raising their young son and hoping for a second child. But with COVID-19 coming, Mast wondered if family time was likely to be in short supply for a while.

Like Ebner, Mast reviewed daily advisories from state and federal agencies on the status of COVID-19 and other health issues. He also conferred regularly with Mark DiMenna, Environmental Health deputy director and a frequent face in the city when discussions turned to mosquitos, bed bugs, and bats. Mast also consulted regularly with staff epidemiologist Kaitlin Greenberg.

"They were already tracking things by the time I got here," Mast said. "In January 2020, the big question was when COVID-19 would get here."

Mast and Ebner were among those city officials gathered February 28, 2020, at the Albuquerque Convention Center along with Mayor Keller, CAO Sarita Nair, COO Lawrence Rael, and other department heads for the situational awareness meeting on COVID-19. It was, Mast said, a crucial meeting and the first of many.

"We knew immediately what each of our agencies knew, what we needed to do, how we might do that," he said. "The specifics would come later, and they would change as the situations arose."

Mast left the meeting convinced that Albuquerque was in good hands.

"From my experience working in this field, I was very impressed at how everybody came together, how quickly everybody was ready to adapt to their roles," Mast said. "We all knew early on that we had to have a cohesive working relationship and that we needed to show the public a cohesive message. We needed that singular voice to the public to gain trust." Keller and his team, Mast said, had that voice and that leadership. "The mayor had to do a lot of myth busting in the beginning because there was so much misinformation or confusion out there and not a lot of guidance coming from Washington, D.C."

Also important was working hand in glove with the state agencies and the office of New Mexico governor Michelle Lujan Grisham. "We were already making those calls with each other," Mast said.

While Mast's office was in city hall, Roger Ebner's office was on the far west side of the city in the Emergency Operations Center (EOC), located in a gleaming, gated citadel off 114th Street where the city's 911 operators and dispatchers for police and fire are also located.

The EOC's main room is a cavernous, fully equipped, secure, state-of-the-art control hub that looks like something out of a Tom Clancy spy thriller. The wall at the front of the room is lined with massive floor-to-ceiling smart boards that display data, maps, charts, news reports from around the world, and whatever other information is relevant to the current crisis. Banks of phones and computers below the screens are divided into four color-coded sections—Operations, Planning, Logistics, and Finance and Administration. A glassed-in conference room, alternatively known as "the fish bowl" or "aquarium," has a panoramic view of the sections and the smart boards and is where officials confer or host the occasional potluck.

Since its opening in September 1999, the EOC has been used for practice disaster drills and a number of real or potential crises such as the Y2K scare, when officials feared a cataclysmic computer meltdown would occur when the year 1999 became 2000, and after September 11, 2001, when the World Trade Center and Pentagon were attacked. In the early weeks of 2020, the EOC was quiet, its incident response at Level 4, the "monitoring" phase when Ebner and a small staff of two remained on standby.

"Level 4 is the day-to-day operations," Ebner said. "It's status quo."

The rise of COVID-19 cases in Washington state in early March 2020 triggered a ramping up to Level 3, the "moderate" phase where a limited local emergency response team is activated at the EOC. For the most part, that team was largely just Ebner and his staff, but with additional monitoring and preparation duties.

"It's when there is a need for a more significant focus on the threat," Ebner explained of Level 3.

In March 2020, EOC staff began acquiring and assessing necessary supplies to tackle the impending health crisis in Albuquerque, including amassing 90,000 N95 masks, more than sixty vaccine transport coolers, and thousands of goggles, gowns, and gloves. Massive refrigerated units in a back room at the EOC were also set to varying chilly degrees in preparation for storing vaccines or medications, should any become available.

With so much advanced preparation, the City of Albuquerque was as ready as it could be with the resources and personnel at hand. Whether that was because of Alan Packman's urgent warning in late February 2020, or because of the steady and seasoned work of disaster pros Roger Ebner and Ryan Mast and their teams, remains a debatable point. It's likely a little of both. What isn't debatable is that the City of Albuquerque was about two weeks ahead of what was coming its way.

And then it came. On March 11, 2020, four New Mexicans became the first in the state to test positive for COVID-19. All four had recently traveled out of state. The state's first cases included a Bernalillo County woman in her seventies who had traveled to the New York City area. None of the first cases had died and all were isolating themselves at home.

It was enough for Governor Michelle Lujan Grisham to declare a public health emergency in New Mexico. In a news conference, she urged people to avoid public gatherings, sanitize common surfaces, and minimize contact with other individuals, even if it meant not attending church and not going anywhere. <app. 1>

"This is a serious situation," Governor Lujan Grisham told reporters. "I will use every tool and resource to keep us safe."

That same day, March 11, the World Health Organization declared COVID-19 a global pandemic. Closures began. The New Mexico state high school basketball tournament, which attracts thousands of exuberant fans and alumni from every corner of the state each March to The Pit in Albuquerque, would go on but without those fans present. The Gathering of Nations, the largest powwow in North America that in April 2019 drew more than 3,000 dancers representing 750 tribes from across the U.S. and Canada to Expo New Mexico in Albuquerque, would be indefinitely postponed in 2020. Albuquerque Academy, a private, college preparatory school, announced that it was shutting down its campus because a member of its community was in close contact with one of the people who tested positive for COVID-19. The next day—March 12, 2020, a Thursday—the state banned all large public gatherings.

The Archdiocese of Santa Fe, which oversees the parishes in Albuquerque and those in the northern and eastern regions of the state, canceled all church services.

On Albuquerque's west side, the EOC was activated, more personnel moved in, and orange tape stripped across the large conference room table in the fish bowl to mark off socially distanced areas between city officials during meetings. By March 12, 2020, the EOC was operating at Level 2, the "major" phase, and it was all hands on deck.

On March 12, 2020, Mayor Keller spoke to the residents of Albuquerque from the EOC, assuring them that they were in good hands and announcing thirty-day closures of the city's KiMo Theater, South Broadway Cultural Center, and the Albuquerque Convention Center, while the ABQ BioPark and Albuquerque Museum—places where people were "transient," moving through and not staying in one place long—would remain open. Other events planned in city facilities were also being considered for closure, while activities such as meals to seniors were being increased. All other city services, especially public safety, would be business as usual in a most unusual time.

It was, as Albuquerque City Council President Pat Davis said, preparedness and not panic.

"We want the public to know that as of right now you can rely on city services as you would before," Mayor Keller emphasized, flanked by Davis, Nair, Rael, Ebner, Mast, and other city government directors, city councilors, and officials from Bernalillo County, Albuquerque Public Schools, and the University of New Mexico Health Sciences Center.

Mayor Activates Emergency Joint information Center. Photo courtesy Mayor's Office, City of Albuquerque.

Mayor Keller meets with city directors at the Joint Information Center, photo courtesy Mayor's Office, City of Albuquerque. Left to right, Mayor Keller, David Simon, Director of Parks and Recreation; Ryan Mast, Director of Environmental Health; Shelle Sanchez, Director of Arts & Culture; Carol Pierce, Director of Family and Community Services; and Anna Sanchez, Director of Senior Affairs; and Sanjay Bhakta, Chief Financial Officer.

Emergency Operations Center before the Mayor's press conference. Photo courtesy Mayor's Office, City of Albuquerque.

"We're as ready as we can be," Keller continued. "We're as prepared as we can be, and we're putting those plans into action."

President Trump had yet to declare a national emergency. That would come on March 13, 2020. Again and again over the course of 2020, the guidance from Trump's White House would be slower and more muddled than public health guidance coming from local government. As coronavirus became an official emergency, and then a global pandemic, some people would come to appreciate that strong close-to-home leadership; others would chafe at what felt like government overreach.

City of Albuquerque CAO, Sarita Nair, became the face of city hall at the EOC, dutifully making the trek from the center of the city to its outskirts over the eerily empty I-40, the digital electronic highway signs flashing advisories urging motorists to stay home.

"I could make the drive in fourteen minutes because there was literally no traffic," Nair said of the commute. "It was so surreal. And because not much was open, you had to remember to bring everything with you, like coffee instead of Starbucks."

Nair was there for a daily meeting, held in the EOC fish bowl, her socially distanced seat at the far end of the large conference table. The meetings were also fed online over Zoom for administrators and directors from other city, state, and federal agencies who were not able to attend in person. Nair, though, preferred being there in person. "So much of what I do is being present."

Mayor Keller and his administration announce new COVID precautions at the Emergency Operations Center. Photo courtesy Mayor's Office, City of Albuquerque.

Each day brought Nair new decisions and new challenges—everything from how full local hospitals were, where to get hand sanitizer for staff, to whether the city was stocked with enough body bags.

"There were a lot of decisions we had to make quickly, and we could do that because we were so well prepared," Nair said.

In the coming days and weeks and then months of 2020, Nair would find herself spending long hours in her office at city hall. Occasionally, she brought Maximus, her black, behemoth Great Dane-boxer mix, so he wouldn't have to spend long nights home alone. Besides the daily EOC sojourn, Nair frequently showed up at the city's larger public facilities such as the BioPark, senior centers, and police headquarters to keep abreast of how things were going and to speak with the employees who kept the city running.

"The biggest decision we had to make was whether we pulled back—whether we furloughed employees or kept them working," Nair said. "But to a person, everybody on the team decided that too many in our community were too vulnerable. They needed the city to keep running, and we needed to keep employees employed, safely and supported. We chose to step up, not step back. That meant ramping up senior meals, childcare, law enforcement, and code enforcement, not curtailing services as some cities had." That decision

Signs at the Albuquerque International Sunport warn of the COVID health order in English and Spanish. Photo by Ramon Penttila, courtesy Albuquerque Museum.

weighed heavily on the CAO. "This was such a big decision and it could be 100% wrong," she said. "We could be putting the lives of our employees in jeopardy."

From her corner office on the eleventh floor, between difficult decisions Nair sometimes caught her breath and just stared out at the breathtaking view of the city she was entrusted with. She and the mayor had joked that her view was better than his, unimpeded by the top floors of the nearby Doubletree Hotel that partly blocked his view of the Sandia Mountains. The view helped remind Nair of what was at stake, as if she needed any reminder. It helped her stay present.

Ryan Mast, over at Environmental Health, would find himself working long hours, too, trying to find a balance between work and family. There would be many days in a row when he would not see his son, asleep when Mast left for work, asleep when he trudged home from work.

"That was pretty tough on my son," he said. It wasn't easy on Mast, either. "But this is what we do, what we prepare for," he said, "and this was something where none of us knew how long it would last."

Mayor Keller prepares to deliver remarks about the city's state of emergency order, March 2020. Photo courtesy Mayor's Office, City of Albuquerque.

The City of Albuquerque provided childcare for essential workers at many of the city's community centers. Photo courtesy Mayor's Office, City of Albuquerque.

City Department of Municipal Development security officers providing security and traffic control at COVID-19 testing sites around the city. Photo courtesy Mayor's Office, City of Albuquerque.

On March 12, 2020, the day Erdrich was to have
appeared in Albuquerque, Mayor Keller announced that
city government was putting safety measures in place
to protect its citizens from whatever COVID-19 would
bring. Those measures included imposing more rigorous
sanitation at public facilities, curtailing city employee
travel out of state, and closing certain city-operated
venues, including the KiMo.

5

Going Dark

It was such a big get. Author Louise Erdrich had been one of the most sought after writers in the national book tour circuit and a longtime favorite of the staff and patrons of Bookworks, one of Albuquerque's last remaining independent bookstores.

Erdrich, a prolific writer whose many books and poems reflect the heritage, hurt, and heart of her Native American experience, was heading out on a twelve-city whirlwind tour throughout the month of March 2020 to promote her new novel, *The Night Watchman*. Albuquerque was the smallest city on the itinerary, which included Boston, Chicago, Houston, and Washington, D.C. That Erdrich had agreed to come to a smaller market was a big deal for Bookworks and a big draw for its A Word with Writers literary fundraiser for the Albuquerque Public Library Foundation.

The fundraiser and reading was scheduled for the night of March 12, 2020, at the KiMo Theatre, an iconic downtown venue at Fifth and Central, whose ornate Pueblo Deco architecture and historical significance had long made the KiMo one of the brightest, most unique spots along Route 66.

"It was such a good event and coming at a great time for us," KiMo manager Larry Parker said. The early part of the year at the KiMo was typically slower. After the annual Ballet Repertory Theatre of New Mexico's production of The Nutcracker completed its well-attended run for the Christmas holidays, the KiMo mostly hosted smaller screenings of classic movie westerns, art shows, and a few theatrical and musical performances until the next major event, the Banff Mountain Film Festival, scheduled for March 13. "The Banff sells out every year," Parker said. "It's one of our biggest events."

The world-renowned Erdrich was set to come the night before the film festival, and once again the 650-seat KiMo had a sold-out show on its hands. It was more good news for the KiMo and for the City of Albuquerque, which purchased the historical building in 1977 and continues to manage it as one of the many venues under the Department of Arts & Culture's umbrella. For each of the past two fiscal years, the KiMo had averaged about three hundred annual events—nearly an event a day.

"For (fiscal year) 2020 through May 12, we were already at 275 events and heading toward a great year," said Parker, who has managed the KiMo since 2008. "We had a lot of stuff going on, a lot of stuff coming in, but we started hearing things." One of those things was COVID-19.

On March 11, 2020, a day before she was to appear in Albuquerque, Erdrich canceled her book signing there and the rest of her book tour.

"Everything changed overnight," Erdrich later wrote on her Facebook page. "But not enough. We have decided to take measures to encourage people to stay home as much as possible." News of her cancellation was posted on her Albuquerque hosts' Facebook pages.

"Bookworks and the Albuquerque Public Library Foundation regret to announce that our event with Louise Erdrich on Thursday night at the KiMo Theatre has just been cancelled at the author's request," one post read somberly. "Ms. Erdrich is returning home to Minneapolis and will reschedule with us at a later date." No one knew how long "later" would be.

On March 12, 2020, the day Erdrich was to have appeared in Albuquerque, Mayor Keller announced that city government was putting safety measures in place to protect its residents from whatever COVID-19 would bring. Those measures included imposing more rigorous sanitation at public facilities, curtailing city employee travel out of state, and closing certain city-operated venues, including the KiMo.

"Everything just stopped," Parker said. The initial closures, Mayor Keller said, were being imposed for thirty days. That gave Parker hope that whatever was happening with this new illness would be dealt with quickly and future event cancellations would be minimal.

"At that time, we figured maybe we would be back in business by Memorial Day," Parker said.

On March 12, 2020, Governor Lujan Grisham had also announced a new state public health order prohibiting mass gatherings of one hundred people or more in New Mexico. That order led to the closures of more entertainment venues, including the 1,985-seat Popejoy Hall at the University of New Mexico Main Campus in Albuquerque, which that night canceled opening night of *Escape to Margaritaville*, a musical featuring Jimmy Buffett songs, and all other events through April 30.

Tricklock Company also postponed the last two weeks of its cutting edge Revolutions International Theatre Festival at its 150-seat venue in downtown Albuquerque, losing ticket money and the travel expenses paid for its international performers. Albuquerque Little Theater, which seats 480,

COVID-19 testing site March 21, 2020. Photo by Jessica Roybal, photo courtesy Albuquerque Museum Digital Archives, object #PA2021.032.002

canceled the second weekend of its production of *Beauty and the Beast*. Expo New Mexico canceled its events. The Santa Ana Star Center in Rio Rancho rescheduled the Foo Fighters concert set for April 14. Santa Fe's Meow Wolf announced the closure of its popular House of Eternal Return and all events and concerts through April 15. Sporting events, including games played by the Albuquerque Isotopes, the city's Minor League Baseball team, and the New Mexico United pro soccer team, then only in its second season, were canceled as well.

Large venues around the country were also shutting down as the coronavirus pushed onward. The National Basketball Association announced it was suspending its season indefinitely as of March 11. On Broadway in New York City, the shows did not go on: every theater went dark March 12.

"When that news came, I realized this was far more serious than I first realized," Parker said. "It just sort of exploded. We didn't know what we were facing."

On March 13, 2020—with 2,700 confirmed COVID-19 cases in the U.S., including ten confirmed cases in New Mexico—President Trump declared a national emergency, still touting the speed with which he'd instituted travel bans and ignoring criticism that his administration had lost precious time by not providing a more coherent federal response to COVID-19, which had seeped into the country in spite of his travel bans, and by the failure to ensure that the U.S. had an adequate supply of COVID-19 tests.

"This will pass," Trump insisted in his address to the nation from the Rose Garden that day. "This will pass through, and we're going to be even stronger for it. We've learned a lot. Tremendous amount has been learned."

Disinfecting the Park, March 20, 2020. Photo by Jessica Roybal, photo courtesy Albuquerque Museum Digital Archives, object #PA2021.032.001

Trump in this address on March 13, also urged every state to immediately set up emergency operation centers. Albuquerque was way ahead of that.

Nearly every day following brought more closures, more emergency health orders. On the same day that Trump declared a national emergency, Governor Lujan Grisham announced that New Mexico K-12 public schools would close for three weeks, effective March 16.

Mayor Keller announced the closures of Albuquerque public libraries, pools, indoor exhibits, and restaurants at the BioPark, the Albuquerque Museum, Explora Science Center, the International Balloon Museum, and Casa San Isidro, a city-run historic farm. City of Albuquerque community centers discontinued events such as bingo and exercise classes but were still open for meal services for seniors and children and certain kid's activities that required pre-registration. City parks remained open, but gatherings of 100 or more people would not be allowed under the state's emergency health orders.

"The bottom line is, stay home if you can," Keller said in a statement on March 13. "We know that not everyone has that choice or ability, and we're making sure seniors and kids get the meals they need, and our first responders are out on the front lines keeping people safe. We are mobilized for the coronavirus response."

Across city government, office workers, including many at city hall, said goodbye to their colleagues, unsure when they might see each other again in the flesh. They changed their voicemail messages to alert callers that they would be working from home for the foreseeable future. Calendars remained on the same date, frozen in time.

More closures came. Restaurants, bars, breweries, eateries, and other food establishments were given one last weekend to conduct business as usual. Under a new State of New Mexico Department of Health emergency order, those same businesses had to begin operating at 50% capacity beginning Monday, March 16. More than six people could no longer sit at a single table, and those tables needed to be at least six feet apart. Patrons could no longer sit at the bar. Four days later, nobody could sit anywhere in any bar, restaurant, or brewery under an even stricter mandate issued by the governor on March 19, 2020.

The Sandia Peak Tramway, which transports about 250,000 passengers every year to breathtaking heights above Albuquerque, was grounded. Also grounded were many of the flights in and out of the Albuquerque International Sunport, which almost immediately saw as much as an 88% decrease in daily boardings from the year before.

"It's an absolute ghost town," Mayor Keller told reporters. "Almost no one is traveling. There are planes leaving our town with one person on them."

Oreste Bachechi, creator of the KiMo Theater. Photo courtesy City of Albuquerque.

By the end of March 2020, a total of 315 people had tested positive for COVID-19 in New Mexico. Five fatalities were reported in the state, including a man in his forties from Bernalillo County who had died alone in his home.

Back at the KiMo Theater, Larry Parker battened down the hatches and finished the grim chore of canceling events. It was sad to think of the people who would not be coming anymore to this remarkable building, the movie palace of Italian immigrant Oreste Bachechi's dreams.

Bachechi had come to the crossroads of Albuquerque in 1885 to seek his fortune, his first venture beginning with a small saloon housed in a tent he pitched near the railroad tracks. From those humble beginnings came a successful wholesale liquor dealership, a grocery store, and a dry goods store run by his wife, Maria. In 1927, the Bachechis welcomed audiences to the KiMo Theatre, a grand and curious spectacle inspired by architect Carl Boller's travels through Acoma and Isleta Pueblos

Pablo Abeita (1870-1940), Governor of the Pueblo of Isleta. Photo by Alabama Milner, c. 1930, courtesy Albuquerque Museum Digital Archives, object #PA1992.005.166

and the Navajo Nation. Newspaper advertisements at the time called the KiMo the "world's foremost Indian theater." Its name, a Tiwa language contraction of sorts for "mountain lion," was suggested by Isleta Pueblo governor, Pablo Abeita, who won $50 in a contest to name the theater.

KiMo Theater, c. 1930. Photo by Brooks Studio, gift of Channell Graham, photo courtesy Albuquerque Museum Digital Archives, object #PA1978.151.856

Patrons marveled at the ornate kiva-like details from the exterior tiling and carvings on the KiMo's exterior to the glowing eyes of buffalo skulls lining the walls inside. On the KiMo's opening night in 1927, guests were entertained by sixty tribal dancers, soprano Margaret Well of the Zuni tribe, Navajo baritone Haske Naswood, and a famous organist from Colorado Springs.

Those early days had been among the good times for the KiMo. Bad times had come along, too. During an afternoon matinee on August 2, 1951, a boiler in the KiMo's lobby had exploded, severely injuring seven movie-goers and killing a six year-old boy named Bobby Darnell. The tragedy, perhaps quite literally, haunted the theater for years to come, with tales told of a ghost resembling a young boy who had an impish penchant for causing trouble unless appeased with doughnuts and toys.

On August 7, 1961, a large fire caused extensive damage to the stage and the front of the auditorium and led to the temporary closure of the KiMo. The KiMo was shuttered again in 1970, unusable anymore as a movie theater, unable to compete with the more modern multiplex cinemas in uptown Albuquerque. Then mayor Harry Kinney made it one of his priorities to save the KiMo, possibly as a performing arts center and certainly as an iconic piece of Albuquerque history. In October 1977, voters approved a $330,000 bond to begin that process. Restoration of the KiMo, now listed on the National Register of Historic Places, was completed in the 1990s as part of a downtown revitalization effort and in time for the seventy-fifth anniversary of Route 66.

Participants in the First American Pageant gather in front of Kimo Theater, August 1931, from Albuquerque Public Library. Photo courtesy Albuquerque Museum Digital Archives, object #PA1978.141.239

The KiMo had survived every crisis, and if it could do that and still be standing after ninety-three years, then surely it could endure a pandemic shutdown for awhile. Surely the words of author Louise Erdrich could be of some comfort as the world careened toward the great unknown.

"I know everyone is experiencing this sense of dislocation, ratcheting between conflicting emotions," Erdrich wrote on her Facebook page on March 19, 2020. "We are all afraid for those we love. But acts of kindness are occurring all around us, ranging from the devotion and heroism of our health workers, to generous deeds that give one heart."

Two months after the KiMo shut down in March 2020, hearts would darken and rage would burn across the country. Peaceful protests in Albuquerque would give way to late-night riots. Fires were set and windows were smashed, and the KiMo was smack in the middle of it all, its survival again in peril. It was enough to break many hearts, including Larry Parker's, who was among those there to pick up the pieces.

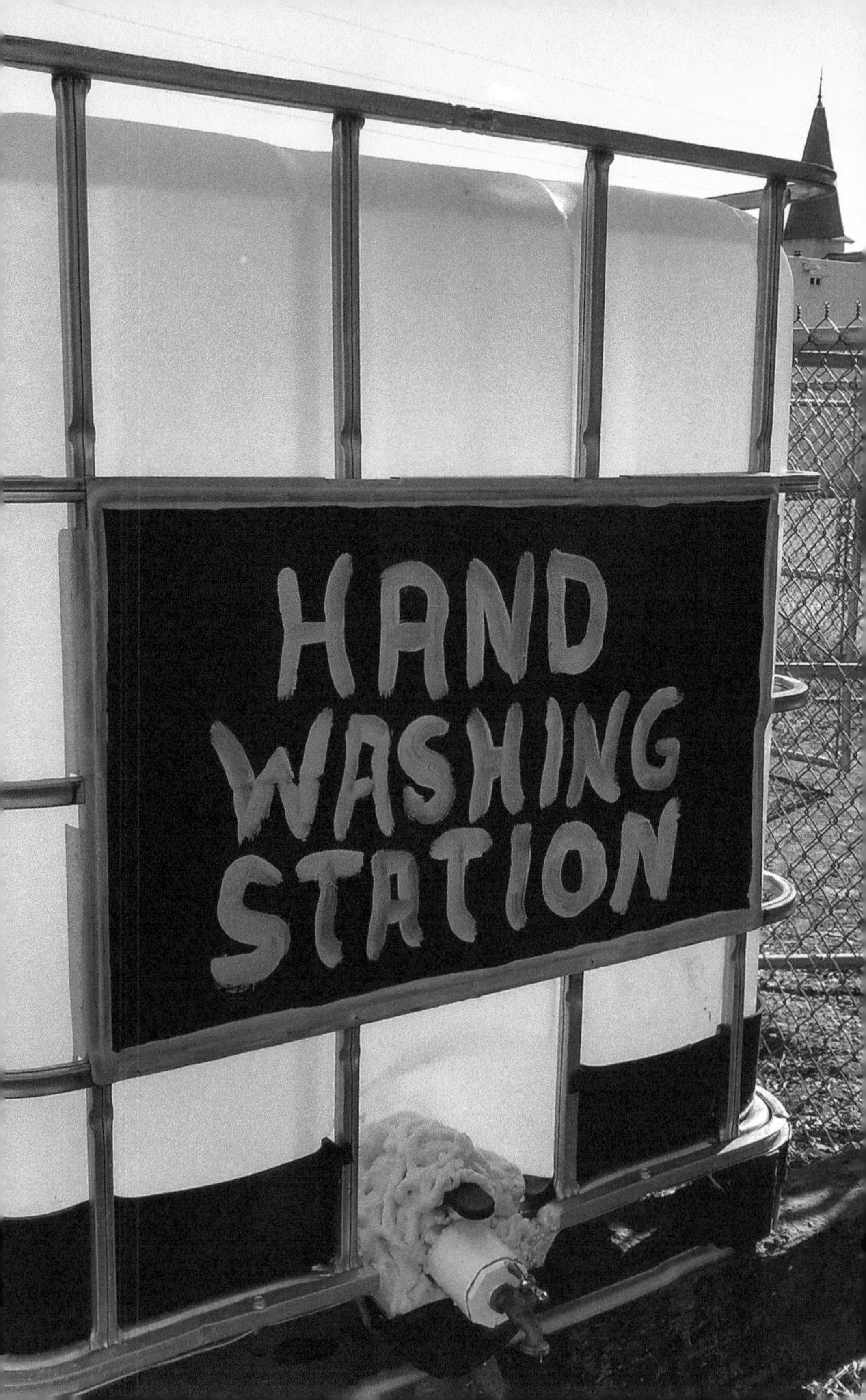
HAND
WASHING
STATION

6

Pulling Together

It was midnight when Nobutoshi Mizushima finally woke up, slumped in a chair after the first full day of business at Ihatov Bread and Coffee, the culmination of years of dreaming and hard work and dough, and it had been a tiring one. Nobu, as people called him, had decided to sit down to rest for a few minutes before heading home after such a busy, exhilarating day. Those minutes had turned into hours and then almost the beginning of the second full day of business.

"Anyway we sold all breads," Nobu wrote on Facebook the next morning. "I bake more today. Please come to visit! We looking forward to see you."

Nobu and his wife, Yuko Kawashiwo, had always dreamed of opening their own place where they could sell the beautiful, bountiful artisan breads and pastries Nobu had become known for during his time at Cloud Cliff Bakery in Santa Fe and at farmers markets in Albuquerque. Owning their own business was the American dream for the Japanese immigrants, and Albuquerque seemed like the perfect place to make that dream a reality. To them, Albuquerque was the city of dreams, the city where people had for centuries turned their ideas, hopes, and meager means into something sustainable, something their own.

Nobu and Yuko found their spot in an abandoned Starbucks in Nob Hill, east of the University of New Mexico along historic Central Avenue on famed Route 66. Before they moved in, their building had housed an Arby's fast food restaurant, famous for its half-barrel yellow roof. Before that, it had been the D&D Buick dealership—the "crossroads for Buick owners from coast to coast"—in the 1950s. Long before that, Nob Hill hadn't been on the crossroads at all.

Nobutoshi Mizushima and Yuko Kawashiwo, owners of Ihatov Bakery. Photo courtesy Jami Seymore, KRQE News, @JamiSeymore on Twitter.

Nob Hill wasn't even "Nob Hill" until 1916 when real estate developer D. B. K. Sellers declared that the tract of land east of UNM should be christened with that name because the area's hilly terrain reminded him of the undulating grades of the swanky neighborhood with the same name in San Francisco. Sellers envisioned swanky here some day.

In its early years, Route 66 bypassed Nob Hill and much of downtown, the UNM area, and the rest of what was then known as the east mesa, depriving the area of the growth opportunities inherent with the Mother Road. Before 1937, Route 66 entered New Mexico's eastern border near Tucumcari and headed west toward Santa Rosa, then north to Santa Fe. From there, the road took a sharp turn south to Albuquerque, skirting the city along what is now Fourth Street and then points west.

The reworking of Route 66 away from Santa Fe and straight through Albuquerque was a boon to development along Central Avenue through Nob Hill and from the Sandia Mountains on the east, to Nine Mile Hill on the west. Weary travelers had their pick in those early days of full-service gas stations and motels such as the De Anza Motor Lodge, Aztec Court, and El Oriente Court. Even after I-40 lured away many of those travelers in the 1980s, Nob Hill remained a vibrant retail area filled with boutiques and eclectic and elegant eateries and bars.

Albuquerque's Nob Hill is one of the few retail areas that remains pedestrian friendly in a city where vehicular travel and big box stores are more

D.K.B. Sellers photo. D.K.B. Sellers and his dog stand beside original Nob Hill sign c. 1940. Photo courtesy Albuquerque Museum Digital Archives, object #PA1978.141.282

the norm now. Beyond the business of Central Avenue are the residential neighborhoods of Nob Hill, the first suburb in Albuquerque. Even today, Nob Hill retains much of its early charm and is filled with historically significant Mediterranean and Pueblo Revival homes, student ghetto bungalows, and the otherworldly creations of Albuquerque architect Bart Prince, all built along tree-lined streets. Nob Hill maintains a village-like appeal, home to older professionals and younger college students. Nobu and Yuko hoped everyone in the neighborhood would embrace them and their ambitious little bakery and coffee shop.

They were off to a good start. In just fifteen days in January 2020, their Kickstarter campaign had raised $16,615, exceeding their goal of $12,000, the estimated amount they needed to open shop. They named their business Ihatov for the magical place described by their favorite author, Miyazawa Kenji.

"Ihatov means utopia, dreamland," Kawashiwo said. "Harmonious." It was all of that for them. Ihatov seemed it was destined to be a magical place for their customers, too.

"When we heard a bread shop was going in, there was a lot of excitement," Nob Hill neighbor Patricia Parkinson said. "We couldn't wait for it to open."

The Guild Theater in Albuquerque's Nob Hill district. Photo by Roland Penttila, 2020, photo courtesy Albuquerque Museum Digital Archives.

Nobu and Yuko turned the building at Central and Tulane Southeast into a welcoming, cozy place where neighbors could linger and chat over a latté and slices of sourdough studded with pear and pepper. Fresh flowers adorned every table, buttery sunlight poured through large glass windows, old wood floors creaked like music, and the room was filled with the intoxicating scents of bread baking and coffee beans roasting. Good spirits also filled the place. Nobu invited a Native American healer to bless the space just before he opened the door for business that first day. Ihatov's first day of business was March 4, 2020.

Even a blessing could not prevent what was coming for the couple's bakery and other businesses, not just in Nob Hill but across Albuquerque and New Mexico and around the globe as COVID-19 began taking its toll. Beginning March 16, 2020, a public health order announced by Governor Lujan Grisham went into effect, restricting all food establishments in New Mexico to operate at 50% capacity, an effort to reduce the spread of COVID-19, which at that point had sickened twenty-one people across the state, fourteen in Bernalillo County. Three days after that, Governor Lujan Grisham ordered all nonessential businesses closed, leaving restaurants and eateries to survive on takeout and delivery and the kindness of customers. It was something Nobu and his wife had never anticipated. No one likely had. Still, they remained optimistic, hopeful that their new neighbors would sustain them during whatever was to come.

"A lot of our customers buy things to go," Kawashiwo said, moments after hearing the governor's announcement. "So maybe for our business it will not be too much affected?"

Four miles east of Ihatov in a grittier neighborhood off Central Avenue, John Bulten wondered how his nonprofit, East Central Ministries, would sustain the people in his community who were already living by threads and good graces and were ill-equipped to protect themselves against an encroaching pandemic.

"For me, it was surreal," said Bulten, executive director and founder of East Central Ministries. The faith-based nonprofit in the International District spreads its mission not by preaching from a pulpit but by reaching out to the community in ways that nurture the body and soul.

"What services could we shut down that would not harm the people we serve?" Bulten wondered.

Almost immediately, he closed the ministry's thrift shop and curtailed its youth programs when the pandemic started, but the ministry's food programs and health clinics remained in operation under limited conditions. They had to. For the people who relied on them, they were essential.

"We had to start thinking about other ways we could help our people weather the COVID-19 storm while keeping all of us safe," Bulten said. "The thing about the International District is that it's a community of people who are front-line workers, immigrants, and those who are on the margins," he said. "Many of our neighbors are people of color who live and die in social inequities every day."

Many are what Bulten refers to as "unsheltered people," not "the homeless," a phrase he feels is dehumanizing and distancing. It is not who they are but something they are experiencing, something that does not have to be permanent. Bulten learned that sentiment in the early days of the ministry in 1999, when he walked the streets of the International District to find out more about the people who live there, what they have, what they need, and how he could live with and work alongside them—not for them. A thoughtful man with a grizzled beard and thousands of miles around the world logged on his hiking boots, Bulten indeed lives alongside those he serves, sharing a 1976 Argosy Airstream with his wife, Morgan Attema, which they gutted and refurbished and parked in the neighborhood.

Across Central Avenue from East Central Ministries stands a low-budget Statue of Liberty, her torch replaced with a street lamp, in the dirt courtyard of the crumbling Bow and Arrow Lodge. The motel was once a bustling Route 66 motor lodge. The Bow and Arrow has since fallen on harder times, repeatedly threatened with closure by the city if its zoning violations aren't addressed and the patrons who pedal in prostitution and narcotics don't move. Lady Liberty arrived sometime after the last city crackdown on the Bow and Arrow in 2019. She is the perfect symbol for a neighborhood a long way from its heyday, a beacon for the tired and the poor, the huddled masses yearning to breathe free.

The iconic Bow & Arrow Lodge sign and the Statue of Liberty in Albuquerque's International District. Photo courtesy Joline Gutierrez Kruger, 2021.

It's a complicated place, the International District, with high poverty, high crime rates, high substance abuse issues, often among a transient population with untreated physical and emotional needs. The International District is also a community rich in culture, its population among Albuquerque's most diverse. This stretch of East Central Avenue is studded with Vietnamese markets and pho shops, authentic Mexican restaurants, and Native American jewelry stores. These neighborhoods are inhabited by people who hold firm to their roots even as they are buffeted about by ceaseless hardships. Albuquerque's International District is its own crossroads of the world.

In 2001, Bulten's East Central Ministries took over and renovated a ramshackle trap house as its main facility. Later, the ministry expanded across the street, adding a small urban farm and a playground along the way. In 2006, the ministry opened One Hope Centro de Vida Health Center, a community-run clinic with three exam rooms and two dental stations where medical personnel see seventy to one hundred patients weekly.

With a deadly pandemic bearing down, the needs of the International District became greater, but providing those needs became harder, and even the simplest things being asked of citizens to protect themselves were hard.

"Washing hands, one of the first things we were told to do to protect ourselves from the virus, is not an easy thing when you are unsheltered and the stores where you once went to use the facilities are closed," Bulten explained.

A community health navigator from the University of New Mexico's Pathways Program partnered with East Central Ministries and started driving around the neighborhood with a five-gallon bucket of water, soap, and towels in the back of her car and stopped for people who wanted to wash their hands. That gave Bulten an idea.

"It was one of those things where we thought, sadly, oh, we should have been doing this all along," Bulten said. "So we had these 275-gallon tanks donated by General Mills for water catchment, and we came up with the idea to fill them with water, attach a liquid soap pump, and put each one on stands as hand-washing stations. It just made a lot of sense."

City government was also interested in assisting with the idea but preferred to wait for a shipment of portable hand-washing stations built specifically for that purpose. But with COVID-19 bearing down, there was no time to wait—not in the International District, anyway.

"Hand-washing stations were rented out across the country and were hard to come by," said Michelle Melendez, director of the City of Albuquerque's Office of Equity and Inclusion, whose duties expanded greatly with each passing day dealing with COVID-19. "Our concern with John's solution for hand-washing stations was the water puddling from the containers. There is no catch basin for water, and we didn't want to create another health problem on top of the initial one." Melendez requested that city Environmental Health Department experts go to the International District to help construct a solution. In the end, pebbles and gravel were added around the stations to help with water drainage.

"John had a great idea and took great efforts to help these people," Melendez said. "We at the city wanted to support him in whatever way we could."

Michelle Melendez, director of Diversity, Equity, and Inclusion. Photo courtesy City of Albuquerque.

In all, East Central Ministries put up sixteen makeshift hand-washing stations, experimenting with different types of soap dispensers and placing most of them on their properties and those of other nonprofits throughout the International District. In addition, Bulten and his team, with the generosity of General Mills, acquired ninety-five hand-washing stations for the Navajo Nation, another community where running water is often a luxury.

"For me, it exposed even more so the tragic lack of our response to the need of many in our communities," Bulten said.

The stations were well-received, and not just for washing hands. Bulten noticed some people used the sites to supply their drinking water, wash their hair, their bodies, their clothes. Some people set up their shelters near the stations, as if they were camping in the wilderness near a water source.

Volunteers and staff of East Central Ministries also began making face masks for its staff and its neighbors.

Hand washing station for public use in the International District. Photo courtesy John Bulten, East Central Ministries.

"Literally, we used any fabric we could find, stuff tucked away in closets, and then we cut pieces of a material similar to what an N95 mask is made with from a big roll we had of it and put that between the layers of the masks," Bulten said. "We reached out to family and friends, donors, everyone."

In the early weeks of the pandemic, it seemed that everybody wanted to find ways to help. Making masks became a practical way to do that. Social groups and individuals with a talent for sewing began stitching up dozens of masks, many given to healthcare workers as supplies of personal protective equipment, or PPE, dwindled. Local JOANN Fabrics and Crafts stores, Superior Alterations, Stitchology, and Ann Silva's Sewing Center offered free scraps of fabric and mask-making kits for those willing to make them. People shared mask patterns on social media, seeking out elastic bands and hair ties to hold the masks in place. One neighbor in Nob Hill hung masks in a tree in the front yard. A note written in chalk on the nearby sidewalk read: "Take mask, wash hands, six feet, love, hope."

Other Albuquerqueans started paying for lunches, pizza, and treats for hospital workers. Residents held drive-by parades at nursing homes to cheer up lonely residents, restricted from having visitors, and in front of the homes of cooped up children celebrating birthdays. Young members of Sandia Baptist Church's College and Career Group volunteered to help seniors with grocery runs, yard work, and other errands. Gift cards from local businesses were purchased to keep them afloat. Blood was donated. Local brewpubs,

Volunteers from East Central Ministries decorate hand washing stations to distribute throughout Albuquerque during the pandemic. Photo courtesy John Bulten, East Central Ministries.

their businesses all but shuttered, turned their efforts to making hand sanitizer for all. NextDoor groups became clearinghouses for those ready to help and those who needed help. Facebook also saw a rise in groups like New Mexico Parents Collaborative Resources, which offered a variety of tips, including how to access federal and local funds to pay rent, how to use Zoom for online meetings, and how to keep children entertained under lockdown.

Tammy Hanks of Albuquerque began encouraging residents to leave larger tips—at least an extra $10—for employees working on the front lines at struggling restaurants and grocery stores who were now tasked with delivering curbside orders. She called her idea the Ubuntu Pledge, derived from an African word that speaks to the connectedness and kindness that exists between people.

"Ten dollars won't break us, and it might make the difference in service workers being able to pay the rent or feed the kids during this crisis," Hanks explained. "Because we are all in this together."

In those early days of the COVID-19 shutdown, residents found ways to reach out to each other even as the world felt more and more isolated. In a time of dread and fear—and anger and disbelief among some—people found kindness, caring, and camaraderie.

The City of Albuquerque found ways to help, too, and to channel the goodwill among its citizens. The city made bus service free for students while

Del Norte High School in Albuquerque hosts a socially-distanced drive-through graduation in May 2020.

schools were shuttered so that they could more easily get Grab-and-Go meals provided by Albuquerque Public Schools.

"Students do not have to go to the school they attend to receive their meals. They only have to access the school site most convenient to them," City of Albuquerque Transit Department director, Danny Holcomb, explained. "Our buses can pick up these students and families closest to where they live and get them to the closest participating site."

The City of Albuquerque's Department of Senior Affairs began collecting nonperishable food, personal hygiene products, and toilet paper—hard to find in the early days of the pandemic—through its Donation Drive for Seniors. The One Albuquerque Fund, along with City of Albuquerque Health and Social Service Centers, began collecting donations to help those in need of temporary housing or who were having trouble paying their rent. Over at the city's westside shelter, residents volunteered to prepare meals for those staying at the shelter.

On March 23, 2020, Governor Lujan Grisham toughened New Mexico's public health orders, issuing a "stay at home" mandate to the public, urging residents to limit all travel, and ordering "nonessential" businesses to close statewide. The orders, the governor explained, were to aggressively minimize person-to-person contact and to ensure spread was mitigated by social distancing and isolation. That day, the New Mexico Department of Health reported that a total of eighty-three people had tested positive for COVID-19, thirty-eight of them in Bernalillo County.

COVID-19 supplies and PPE arrive for distribution in Albuquerque. Photo courtesy Mayor's Office, City of Albuquerque.

City of Albuquerque free COVID-19 supply distribution. Photo courtesy Mayor's Office, City of Albuquerque.

Mayor and First Lady Keller help with the distribution of City of Albuquerque "Grab and Go" meals. Photo courtesy Mayor's Office, City of Albuquerque.

On March 24, six days after he had declared a public health emergency in Albuquerque, Mayor Keller wrote a personal note to the city of Albuquerque to convey his thanks for a community that seemed more united than ever.

"For all of us in the Duke City, the past few weeks are changing our lives. Like me, it may even be hard to recall what daily life was like just days ago," he wrote. "I am inspired daily by the outpouring of compassion in our community to help those most in need, and how we have risen to this fight with courage, resolve, and determination." Mayor Keller promised to uphold his end in the fight, vowing to keep the public informed of his administration's response to the pandemic, and to keep the city running.

"I will continue to fight to keep you safe, while making sure that people are still receiving the necessary services that they need during this uncertain time," he wrote. "Stay strong, Albuquerque."

The next day, March 25, 2020, New Mexico announced its first coronavirus death—an Eddy County man. He would not be the last.

As the pandemic wore on, kindness and patience began to wear thin. Businesses began to fail, unable to hold on, despite millions in city, state, and federal funds freed up to tide them over. Tempers flared. Skepticism grew. Discord, even among city police, rose. Among those taking the brunt of that discord were the employees from City of Albuquerque's Constituent Services.

"For the most part, these employees are young and idealistic. They're enthusiastic, the school spirit of city hall, and they're listening to some of the angriest constituents," CAO Sarita Nair said. "That took its toll."

Nair, whose job in part, she says, is to empower others in their jobs, called about twenty of the employees of Constituent Services into a conference room at city hall. She could feel the heaviness of their discouragement and fatigue. Nair offered them her support and her shoulder and reminded them of a truism: if you're not crying at least once a week, you're probably doing it wrong. She assured them they were doing it right and that someday everything would be all right. She hoped that she was right.

Over the next months, CAO Nair, Mayor Keller, and their team kept looking for how to do things right, putting out fires—literally on the summer night when downtown Albuquerque burned—and seeking ways to keep the city running under difficult conditions, all while trying not to furlough a single city employee.

The Keller administration also helped hundreds of mom-and-pop shops stay afloat by distributing small business grants. Among the recipients was Ihatov Bread and Coffee in Nob Hill, where Nobu was still baking, still hoping. Under the governor's orders, his bakery was still allowed to conduct delivery and carryout business. Nobu and Yuko had known hard times before. They didn't have much to live on, but they always had sourdough. They always had faith that their dream would not fail. As the days of the COVID-19 shutdown continued, they learned that their new community would not let them fail.

Regularly, almost like clockwork, a man from the neighborhood showed up and bought at least $100 worth of baked goods—a welcome jolt to the Ihatov business but a lot of dough for one person to purchase. The bread buyer did not disclose his name or why he needed so much bread, but his neighbors, including Patricia Parkinson, knew who he was and what he was doing with so much bread.

"I had gone over to his house, and he was in the process of bagging all this bread," Parkinson said. "And then he hands me a bag to take home with me, and it was still hot and so good." What her neighbor did was so good.

"He just decided he was going to help out this little store and then help out his neighbors," she said. "It was such a lovely gift." But it was more than that. "Something like that just makes me hopeful," Parkinson said. "We are all looking for emotional safety, especially in these scary, isolated, uncertain times and a world that was already lacking in communication. A simple thing like bread between neighbors offers us a little of that, a little of the reminder that we are all in this together and can pull together."

There, on the crossroads of Albuquerque in the midst of a pandemic, a small but significant bit of utopia, a dreamland, survived.

Mural celebrating the pandemic's healthcare heroes in Albuquerque's Nob Hill neighborhood. Photo by Roland Penttila, courtesy Albuquerque Museum.

7

Learning Curve

Matthew Whelan walks faster than he talks, striding through the labyrinth of offices and briskly greeting employees that he sails past at the Solid Waste Department in an industrial swath of Albuquerque's North Valley. It's the only way to get the lay of the land, the way he prefers to check in with staff in this sprawling and circuitous facility, whose dated exterior likely hasn't changed much since 1960 when it was the N.C. Ribble Company heavy equipment plant.

Before dawn, Whelan hears the drivers and supervisors arriving, their jovial chatter blending with the clanking of blue lockers where they stash their belongings, the ice clattering from the dispenser into coolers and thermoses and Big Gulp cups, the click of the time clock. Someone blasts a radio. Supervisors stand at their podiums in the center of the room, doling out the route sheets. This is the social scene of Solid Waste, the gathering place for coworkers, most of whom won't see each other again during the workday until they return to the locker room to grab their things and clock out.

Photos over the years capturing milestones at Solid Waste—a retirement, an award, a wedding announcement, a farewell to a coworker who has passed away—have often been taken in that locker room, its distinctive checkerboard floor of sky blue and gray linoleum spreading in the background like a giant gingham picnic cloth.

Theirs is a thankless job, a physically grueling job. The so-called "garbage man" is the fifth most dangerous job—and the top dangerous municipal job— in the U.S., ranked well above police officers, according to *Industrial Safety and Hygiene News*. Sanitation workers are exposed to potentially dangerous materials tossed in trash bags. They contend with poor driving conditions

Director of Solid Waste Management, Matthew Whelan, promotional shot for YouTube show, "Talkin' Trash Tuesday." Photo courtesy Solid Waste Department, City of Albuquerque.

caused by inclement weather and inept drivers. Long routes and long hours can lead to poor dietary habits and fatigue. Theirs is also a crucial job. The city needs its police officers and firefighters to keep it safe, certainly. Sanitation workers not only keep the city safe but livable and clean and functioning.

Whelan, named director of the Solid Waste Department by Mayor Tim Keller in early 2018, has long been enamored of the solid waste business, finding treasure in trash since he was a kid working for his grandfather's company, Silva Sanitation, in Las Cruces. Calling the department "Solid Waste Management" has never felt right to Whelan. If he had his way, he would consider changing the name to the "Clean City Department," expanding on the title of one of its divisions.

"Solid waste is only a portion of what we manage," Whelan said. "We're the folks who handle the recycling, the cleaning of the street medians, and the removal of graffiti."

Change beyond a name has been in the works for years at Solid Waste. At the current site on Edith and Comanche Northeast alone, a new eighteen-bay vehicle maintenance facility is planned, as is a new 20,000 square-foot, two-story administration building. A customer rate increase from back in fiscal year 2015 is providing the funding for the new digs.

Days after taking office in 2017, Mayor Keller nixed controversial plans by the previous administration to plop a garbage transfer station on the Edith site. Neighbors balked. Keller listened. The transfer station plans vanished, and so did the $4 million already spent in preparation and planning for it. What remained were the plans for the new maintenance facility and administrative building, which will replace both the labyrinth and the locker room. Whelan inherited those upcoming changes. He'd spent months strategizing the best way to accommodate his employees and keep the department running while the new facility was being built, and the old one was demolished. Then COVID-19 came and trashed those plans.

Whelan had seen coronavirus coming.

"I heard about it on the news one day, I don't remember when, but I knew it was just a matter of time," he said. "It was like red dots on a map and the dots keep multiplying and gathering and spreading closer and closer into one big blotch." With COVID-19 on the scene, Whelan laid aside the plans for the new construction to focus on keeping the Solid Waste Management Department functioning.

City of Albuquerque COO Lawrence Rael said he was impressed with Whelan's quick thinking.

"We as a city had already started triaging how to keep the city running, what services needed to keep being offered, who needed to be at work and who could be at work, and it really was something daunting to imagine," Rael said. "It was obvious from the start that trash collection still needed to happen, and we needed to figure out how to do that safely and keep our workers safe. One of the first directors who just jumped into it all was Matt."

One early morning in March 2020, Whelan sent his supervisors and staff out with a mission: buy bandanas, cloth, anything to make masks. Buy hand sanitizer in bulk, bleach, spray bottles, small bottles, wipes, laptops, and toughbooks.

"Buy as many supplies as you can, everything you can think of, everywhere you can think of," he told them. "Walmart. Dollar Store. Boot Barn. Everywhere."

Whelan pulled one employee off of his regular duties after hearing he did upholstery on the side and assigned him to make hundreds of masks—150 a day. While many may have expected—or hoped—that a shutdown might last a few months, Whelan told his staff to prepare for a longer siege lasting a year, maybe two.

"This thing is not going to go away fast," Whelan told them. "Think of it as what I call the restaurant system, like when a hostess tells you it's a forty-five minute wait, and it turns out to be thirty and you're happy, but when it's an hour you're unhappy. Prepare for that fifteen minutes, and hope for less but prepare for the worst."

Offices at Solid Waste became storage rooms for supplies. Desks became workstations to fill sixty-nine-cent plastic travel bottles with hand sanitizer from five-gallon jugs and plastic spray bottles with solutions of bleach. Office employees packed hundreds of shopping bags, one for each driver, with the bottles, a roll of paper towels, a mask or bandana, wipes.

On March 15th, 2020, Albuquerque City Council passed an act amending city government's emergency powers to incorporate public health. Three days later, on March 18, 2020, Mayor Keller declared a public health emergency in the city (app.2). By then, the Solid Waste Department had already spent the two previous weeks preparing for whatever came its way.

"We were ahead of the curve," Whelan said. Nevertheless, given the unknown nature of the pandemic, pivots in city government were hard to predict. "Sometimes it felt like we were making it up as we went."

He still had the hardest tasks ahead, though. For one, Whelan had to send almost all of his office staff home, providing laptops to those who needed one so they could continue to do their jobs remotely. He also had to shut down all common spaces, restrooms, and the drivers' locker room at Solid Waste. The time clock to punch in and out, vending machines, and the ice machine were all off limits, too. Suddenly, Whelan's walk through the labyrinth at Solid Waste was like walking through a ghost town.

Drivers still had to do their jobs, however. They were essential workers. Trash wasn't going to pick itself up on its own. If anything, the volume of residential trash was bound to increase as more people hunkered down in their homes under the lockdown. With 217 drivers covering 540 residential, and also all commercial and recycling routes, it was a massive task. Whelan and his team devised a plan to have drivers begin their day in their trucks instead of in the locker room, checking in remotely with their supervisors for their route sheets via laptop and toughbook. They were given the bags with hand sanitizer and masks, makeshift, made, or otherwise. They were instructed to wipe down the interiors of their trucks with disinfectant before and after their shift.

Drivers were placed on route-based schedules instead of the usual hourly pay system, which meant that they still got paid for an eight-hour day even if they finished their day earlier. It was one way, Whelan said, to keep drivers safe, to keep morale up, and to provide something akin to hazard pay.

Whelan had been right about the increase in residential trash tonnage. In April 2020, his drivers collected 14% more trash on residential routes than they had the previous year. In contrast, his commercial route drivers were collecting 23% less trash as businesses across the city shut down under the state's public health orders.

"So we had to keep making changes and adjusting our drivers and routes to make things work," Whelan said. "It was a shifting situation."

Despite all Whelan's efforts, many drivers were angry and unnerved, unhappy that they were being sent into the great, potentially dangerous unknown like expendable guinea pigs.

"There was a lot of upset, a lot of fear about how they were going to stay safe," Whelan said. "A lot of 'I hear that it's this or it's that.' A lot of worry about touching trash and cans and everything out there. A lot of just being out there. The airborne aspect. There was so much we didn't know."

Navigating the pandemic was certainly a learning curve, and Whelan's department was hardly alone.

"We had to figure out how to do all these things because of something we had never known or experienced," said Dr. Shelle Sanchez, director of the City of Albuquerque's Arts & Culture Department. Her staff was tasked with coming up with ways to salvage, if possible, the many city-sponsored concerts

City of Albuquerque's most essential workers, the "garbage men." Photos courtesy Solid Waste department, City of Albuquerque.

and events, from Albuquerque Summerfest to the Twinkle Light Parade, during COVID-19. "We had no idea how long this would last," Sanchez admits.

Among the city departments that needed to figure out quickly how to fulfill its duties was Senior Affairs, whose clients were among the most vulnerable and the most at risk from both COVID-19 and the shutdown of services. More than ever, the department had to serve as a safety net. On March 17, 2020, director of Senior Affairs, Anna Sanchez, and her staff were forced to shut down the department's programs and activities at the City of Albuquerque's eight senior and multigenerational centers, fitness centers, and eleven satellite meal sites. Senior Affairs quickly shifted their efforts by expanding home-delivered meal service and establishing six drive-up Grab and Go sites across the city. The department also conducted wellness visits to check on homebound seniors and found ways to continue helping seniors get to essential appointments.

To CAO Sarita Nair, what made the COVID-19 learning curve seem steeper was how good things had been before they went bad.

"Everything was going great in our first years before the pandemic. The economy was better and we were on track with many of the mayor's visions

Director of Senior Affairs, Anna Sanchez, at a "Grab and Go" meal distribution during the pandemic. Photo courtesy City of Albuquerque Department of Senior Affairs.

for the city," Nair said. "It was not like we were standing still, and then got hit by a train; it was like we were dancing, and then got hit by a train."

City council meetings carried on, not in council chambers at city hall as usual but via Zoom, the new COVID-safe way to hold meetings and news conferences online. For some, the learning curve was steep. In meetings in spring 2020, some councilors struggled to find camera angles on their computers that didn't cut off half their faces or peer deeply into their cavernous nostrils. Others struggled with poor internet connections that froze their images on the screen or garbled their words. Councilors forgot to unmute themselves.

One city official who quickly got the hang of Zoom meetings and videos and the new ways to rely on remote communication in the midst of a pandemic was Matthew Whelan. Ever the solid waste management ambassador, he began creating short, goofy but informative videos to educate the public on what the solid waste department does and what the public can do to keep the city clean. It was a way to reach Albuquerque residents when more conventional ways such as appearing on local morning TV talk shows or guest speaking at community events were no longer available to him.

Whelan called the videos "Talkin' Trash Tuesdays" and posted them on Keep ABQ Beautiful's pages on YouTube and Twitter. A spoof on *Mr. Rogers' Neighborhood* in which Whelan sings the theme song and dons a sweater, became a lesson on keeping the neighborhood clean. Whelan as rapper Flavor "Flava" Flav, wearing a large clock dangling from a gold-chain necklace, reminded residents that a trash pick-up isn't missed until after 5:30 p.m. that day. Mayor Keller, still recognizable in a shaggy blond wig and nerdy glasses, joined in as Garth for a *Wayne's World* sendoff about illegal dumping.

Screenshot from "Talkin' Trash Tuesday," "Wayne's World" episode, with Mayor Tim Keller. Courtesy Solid Waste Department, City of Albuquerque.

Citizens take part in City of Albuquerque's "Clean City" initiatives, while observing COVID-19 best practices. Photo courtesy Solid Waste Department, City of Albuquerque.

"People don't really know everything we do at the Solid Waste Department," Whelan said. "We're trying to educate the public on everything we do in whatever way we can."

As the pandemic continued to spread, those videos became not only a fun way to learn about keeping the city clean, but also a reminder that sometimes it's just nice to keep laughing, even during a pandemic.

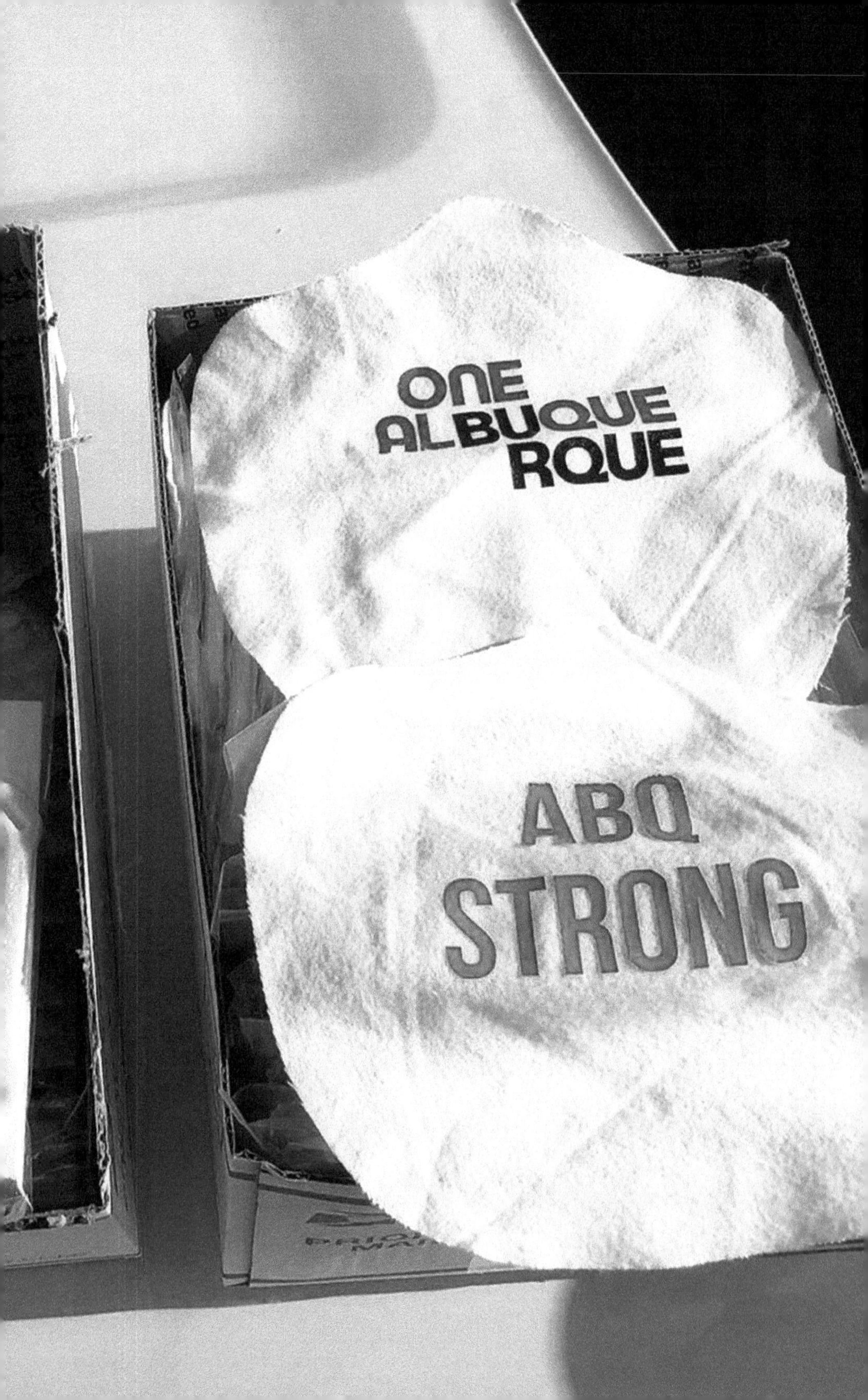
ONE
ALBUQUE
RQUE
ABQ
STRONG

8

The Cavalry Arrives

It was supposed to be a quick favor. Luke Esquibel, coordinator for the University of New Mexico Albuquerque unit of the Medical Reserve Corps, had been out at the city's Westside Emergency Housing Center trying to keep the hundreds of folks there healthy and safe from the onslaught of COVID-19 when he got the call in April 2020.

Esquibel was used to being called into action for the Medical Reserve Corps wherever he was needed, for missions big and small. The corps enlists volunteers to step in when the medical workforce needed more hands on deck for such tasks as manning flu shot clinics and providing care for immigrants, homeless people, and displaced victims at Red Cross shelters.

"We were one of the first fourteen corps in the country, begun here twelve or thirteen years ago by Dr. Paul Roth," he said, referring to the former chancellor of the University of New Mexico Health Sciences Center and dean of the School of Medicine. "We're something of an emergency health support group, a force multiplier."

Besides working out at the Westside Emergency Housing Center, aka the westside shelter, Esquibel had last been called into action in March 2020 when a late-season snowstorm stranded truckers and motorists along I-40. He and other volunteers were ferried out to Moriarty, forty miles east of Albuquerque, by New Mexico State Police to render aid to the motorists. In New Mexico, the Corps has been activated many times but never for a major disaster. Then came COVID-19, and the Corps became even more indispensable.

"We're New Mexico's best kept secret in the fight against COVID," Esquibel said.

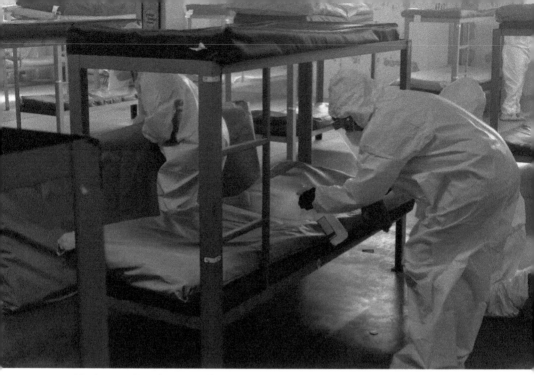

Workers sanitize the Westside Emergency Housing Center during the spring of 2020.

New Mexico Medical Reserve volunteer, Luke Esquibel, courtesy Luke Esquibel.

Luke Esquibel with First Lady Liz Keller pre-COVID. Photo courtesy Mayor Keller @ MayorKeller on Facebook.

The quick favor corps head Bobbie MacKenzie asked of Esquibel was to train staff at the Hilton Garden Inn near the Albuquerque International Sunport on the proper use of personal protective equipment, or PPE. The airport Hilton was being prepared as one of five "wellness hotels," this one for people who had tested positive for COVID-19 and needed to isolate but were not sick enough to be hospitalized. The wellness hotels were also for patients discharged from the hospital after recovering from COVID-19 who still needed to isolate because they had no adequate home to return to. Other wellness hotels were in the works to house first responders or people who were homeless and no longer able to stay at the westside shelter, because of the shelter's reduced capacities under COVID-19 restrictions.

The favor seemed easy enough, especially for Esquibel, whose full-time job was with UNM training folks on the use of PPE, cardio-pulmonary resuscitation techniques, and other basic emergency medical care. He showed up at the hotel dressed in casual clothing.

Hotel general manager, Brittany Lujan, looked confused. She had clearly not been informed that Esquibel was coming.

"Can you please repeat your name and what you're doing here?" Lujan asked Esquibel.

He did, but her look of confusion remained.

What PPE? What training? "Is this about the COVID people here?" Lujan asked.

Esquibel froze. "Wait, what did you say?" he asked.

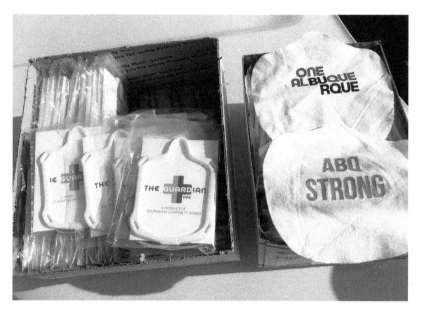

PPE, personal protective equipment with the City of Albuquerque's "One Albuquerque" pledge. Photo courtesy Mayor's Office, City of Albuquerque.

"The sick people with COVID," she responded. "We have five of them here."

No COVID-19 patients were supposed to be at the hotel yet. The hotel had no PPE, no protocols for how to safely deal with the patients, and no protection for any of them. Oh crap, Esquibel thought. This is bad.

"We've got some work to do," he told Lujan, wishing he had worn hospital scrubs rather than casual clothes, wishing he had prepared to spend a far longer time at the hotel than he had anticipated. This was no quick favor, but the cavalry, in the guise of one Luke Esquibel, was here.

"No one knew this was going to happen—not yet anyway and not like this," Esquibel said. "What we didn't have were specific protocols in advance. You can't throw sand in the air and expect it to turn into a castle."

Esquibel knew this wellness hotel gig was going to be a full-time job—more than full time. This wasn't like volunteering after work on the weekends at the westside shelter or spending a few hours in the cold with stranded truckers. Esquibel was a volunteer, not getting paid, but it didn't matter. He was here to make sure that this COVID-19 mission didn't become a disaster. He contacted McKenzie to fill her in and had her scrounge together as much PPE—masks, gloves, gowns—as could be found for the hotel. He requested more corps volunteers and others to provide patient care and to perform whatever tasks were needed—from transporting food and PPE to answering phones.

The COVID-19 patients already on site at the Hilton had simply walked through the front door and into the lobby to be checked in. "Well, we're stopping that right now," Esquibel said. He ordered the front door of the hotel locked and manned by a security guard. Hospitals and other agencies were asked to call before dropping off patients. Those patients were then escorted away from common areas such as the lobby to an isolated, sanitized area to be checked for symptoms and checked in to what folks nicknamed "the COVID Hotel."

"Our whole objective as soon as the patients got off the bus was to determine whether they were well enough for us to treat them," Esquibel said.

Of top importance was keeping everybody safe, especially the hotel staff that chose to remain. Housekeeping staff still had to clean the rooms after a patient was discharged and get it ready for the next patient. It was a constant churn.

"The hotel workers were scared," Esquibel said. "They're a vulnerable population." Staff were also willing to help, though.

"Other hotels were having trouble keeping staff, but here they wanted to say that they played a role in the safety of the people and the community during COVID-19," Esquibel said. "They wanted to be a part of the fight against the coronavirus."

Hotel staff were taught how to put on and take off PPE and how to sanitize themselves and the rooms using CDC protocols. City of Albuquerque Environmental Health employees arrived to help train staff with the best cleansers to use in the rooms, the best way to wash bed linens and towels, and the best way to vacuum the rooms to mitigate the spread.

COVID-19 public health messages from the City of Albuquerque Environmental Health Department.

"None of us knew then how the disease was transmitting, so we took every precaution to protect the housekeeping staff," said Michelle Melendez, the city's director of equity and inclusion, whose role during the pandemic greatly increased because of her unique background as a former State of New Mexico Department of Health employee. As COVID-19 set in, Melendez activated her expertise in emergency response, becoming the point person for the wellness hotels, among other duties. Melendez was a valuable asset to Esquibel.

"She's the person who can make things happen," he said. Melendez and Esquibel had worked together about two years before with asylum seekers at the Mexican border. In Esquibel, Melendez knew she had a good leader.

"The Medical Reserve Corps really came through," Melendez said, "and it started with Luke."

Esquibel was named operations chief at the hotel, a job consuming so many hours that the days blurred into each other, seven days a week.

"Someone had to be on hand to check in busloads of as many as thirty people discharged by hospitals in the middle of the night," he said. "Someone had to be there when a fever spiked."

The state's Emergency Operations Center contacted Esquibel's supervisors at UNM and asked them to allow him to take a leave of absence so that he could manage the hotel full time. With most classes shut down, he wasn't doing a lot of teaching anyway. UNM agreed but on an unpaid basis. Later that month, the City of Albuquerque received $150 million through the federal CARES Act, and that provided much of the funding to pay Esquibel a salary and for the cost of running the wellness hotels. The city also provided the wellness hotels with personnel borrowed from other city departments whose activities were mostly curtailed by the pandemic shutdown. On any given day, wellness hotels were staffed by employees from the City of Albuquerque Senior Affairs Department, Community Events Division, city pools, and the Balloon Museum, among other unlikely helpers. Employees from Bernalillo County departments also took their turns working, doing whatever was necessary, from answering phones to passing out meals.

"At first they were scared, which was understandable," Esquibel said, "but we found ways to keep them safe. If I needed supplies, they ordered them. They made arrangements to transport people and items. It was a way to keep them on the job when their regular jobs weren't happening. It was a win-win."

Volunteers also came from the University of New Mexico Hospital, First Nations Health Clinic, local homeless services and shelters such as Healthcare for the Homeless and Heading Home, and even school nurses from Albuquerque Public Schools. They were all needed. From the first day Esquibel walked in the door and got the wellness hotel up and running, the hotel's 107 rooms were almost always filled. It was quite a mix of occupants, as well, definitely not your typical tourist clientele. Many of the patients came from homeless shelters or the streets. Some came from pueblos and the Navajo reservation. Some came from halfway houses. Some were truckers from other states who had gotten sick on the road through New Mexico. The hotel also accepted "persons under investigation," or PUI, people who exhibited COVID-19 symptoms but were awaiting test results. That required setting up a line of communication with the state laboratory to obtain results rapidly.

So much work had to be done. It was like reinventing the wheel while the wheel was rolling. Arrangements needed to be made to bring in patients' prescription medications, oxygen tanks, methadone. Patients needed to be

Mayor Keller was among many city employees who delivered free meals to seniors in May 2020. Photo courtesy Mayor's Office, City of Albuquerque.

A city employee distributes meals at a community center. Photo courtesy Mayor's Office, City of Albuquerque.

convinced to remain inside their rooms, alone, for days, only being rotated safely outside for a few minutes to "stretch" their lungs. Residents from pueblos, even after they tested negative for COVID-19, had to be told they could not go home because their communities were prohibiting people from entering their boundaries. Protocols were devised, then discarded, as the days wore on and situations changed almost constantly. Esquibel and his team had a motto: "That was two seconds ago."

In the beginning of the pandemic, the hotel hadn't even planned for how they would feed their patients. The Hilton's Garden Grill and Bar, which only served breakfast and happy hour drinks before the pandemic, was closed, as was the Pavilion Pantry, which had sold snacks and drinks. Less than half a mile away from the Hilton, the larger, full-service Sheraton Albuquerque Airport Hotel sat mostly empty, its Left Turn at Albuquerque restaurant forced to reduce its capacity to just 25%. Esquibel contacted the Sheraton's chef and kitchen staff and got them to agree to prepare three meals a day for the patients at the Hilton, even providing a daily menu from which patients could select their preferences.

"That allowed their kitchen folks to keep working, and it kept our patients fed," Esquibel said.

Despite the successes, issues cropped up at the wellness hotel. Toilets clogged, water leaked, and precautions had to be taken to keep plumbers safe enough to go into patients' rooms to make repairs. One patient demanded she be allowed to order takeout food because of food allergies. Esquibel said he attempted to accommodate her, but then she told ten other patients and they, too, suddenly developed allergies and demanded takeout. Some patients who knew each other from a halfway house were unruly, Esquibel said, refusing to follow hotel rules, wanting to hang out together in a room to smoke rather than remain isolated in their own rooms. They requested liquor be delivered to them. Pizza and beer. Esquibel told them no. After five days, those patients were moved to a different setting.

Then there was a mother from Africa who had given birth to a baby and fallen sick with COVID-19. The woman, who could only speak Swahili, and her baby, had to isolate in a room. She had ten children on the outside, and several of them showed up regularly at the hotel with food for their mother. Each time, they begged to see their mother and their new sibling.

"They had never seen the baby," Esquibel said, turning them away. "It was heartbreaking."

On Mother's Day, he quietly arranged for a visit between the woman and her children. Esquibel had the mother come outside with the baby and stand at a distance from her older children, who all wore masks. It was a touching moment during a very hard time.

"We wanted to keep them happy," Esquibel said.

Esquibel just wanted to keep going, tired from the stress and long hours but energized by the challenge and the chance to help people. Each day began early with rounds and meetings, checking patients in, checking patients out,

Albuquerque Police Department demonstrates proper use of PPE and social distancing. Photo courtesy APD @abqpolice on Twitter.

putting out fires, plugging up leaks, and keeping people happy. Around 5 p.m. on some evenings, when things quieted down, Esquibel left the hotel in the hands of a few dependable nurses, so he could take some personal time to go home. The process took a series of clothing changes—out of scrubs at the hotel, into sweats for the drive home, into different clothes in an anterior room in the house he shares with his older brother, then out of those clothes to take a shower, and into new ones afterward. He washed the clothes before relaxing for a couple of hours then heading back to the hotel that night, working until midnight, or later, if necessary. It wasn't an easy schedule.

"There were times when I wanted to say, 'why the hell am I doing this? Why can't I do this on Zoom?'" he admitted. "But that was two seconds ago."

Esquibel stayed on as operations manager at the wellness hotel at the Hilton Garden Inn until the end of June 2020, the favor lasting three months. The Medical Reserve Corps, meanwhile, had grown from a little more than 1,000 members to about 7,400 members as the pandemic raged on. Esquibel went back to teaching at UNM in July 2020, but his experience at the wellness hotel had been so intense that it was hard to shake it off, hard to remember what reality was outside the hotel, hard to remember how or what to teach.

"Take a couple of days off, remember what you used to know," Esquibel's supervisor at UNM advised him. He did. "I can laugh about it now, but it was shocking to go back to a regular job," Esquibel said.

His service with the corps in the war against COVID-19 wasn't over yet. In November 2020, Esquibel was activated again to set up an alternate care site at the old Lovelace Gibson Medical Center, not far from the airport or the Hilton Garden Inn where he started Albuquerque's first COVID-19 wellness hotel. The site was to accommodate patients recovering from coronavirus who still needed additional oxygen to breathe. This time, Esquibel got a head start before patients started to arrive.

As Memorial Day weekend neared in 2020, COVID-19 was still taking its toll, slower but surely now in Bernalillo County, which accounted for 1,464 cases out of the 7,624 cases across New Mexico.

9

Cruel Months

It was likely just wishful thinking, but in early April 2020 it seemed possible that the COVID-19 nightmare might be short-lived thanks to the sacrifices Americans were making to stay home, stay apart, wear masks, and wash hands—even if they had only done so for less than one month.

Maybe President Trump was right when at a rally in New Hampshire in February 2020 he had predicted that as temperatures warmed in April the coronavirus would "miraculously" go away. He envisioned packed churches on Easter, which in 2020 fell on April 12, and an economy that would quickly roar back with the reopening of businesses and the restoration of normalcy.

Mayor Tim Keller was optimistic about reopening Albuquerque, too, but carefully, slowly, and with science as the guide. Likely not in April, he thought.

"We do hope it's weeks as opposed to months, but the virus picks the date," Mayor Keller said.

By the first week in April 2020, it was clear that the virus was not ready to pick a reopening date. The number of positive tests for COVID-19 in New Mexico stood at 543. Of those, 225 were in Bernalillo County. Eleven people had died statewide.

By Easter, April 12, 2020, the number of positive tests had more than doubled, with 1,345 cases statewide, 455 in Bernalillo County, and thirty-one deaths. Churches that day were not packed as they usually were. Annual pilgrimages that draw tens of thousands to local sites El Santuario de Chimayó in northern New Mexico and Tomé Hill south of Albuquerque were discouraged. The University of New Mexico's football stadium that in normal years attracts more than 20,000 worshippers for Calvary Church's sunrise services remained empty.

Two weeks later, by the end of April 2020, New Mexico's COVID-19 numbers had blown up: 3,411 reported cases, 812 in Bernalillo County, and 123 dead. COVID-19 was growing faster than springtime flowers.

At his daily briefings, streamed live on Facebook since the earliest days of the lockdown, Mayor Keller assured residents of Albuquerque that city government continued to be well prepared and adequately funded to handle the pandemic.

So far, the financial losses to Albuquerque caused by the pandemic shutdown were not as devastating as had been feared. Gross receipts tax distribution—levied on the sale of most goods and services and the lifeblood of the city budget—remained relatively steady, thanks in part to monthly internet sales tax revenue that the city had only begun collecting the previous summer. Increased construction, the initial panic-shopping frenzy for toilet paper and other staples, and the bolstering of incomes thanks to the federal stimulus checks and unemployment bonuses also helped the bottom line.

"We're doing pretty well, comparatively speaking," Keller said. "For a large city, Albuquerque is actually doing pretty good." Mayor Keller could also proudly proclaim that he had not had to furlough any City of Albuquerque employee from any department. In addition, city government had received $150 million from the federal CARES Act and from state and local dollars freed up to help small businesses and folks unable to pay their rent. By April 2020, the One Albuquerque Fund had already given out $50,000 in donations for emergency housing and was about to hand out another $50,000 to the city's micro-business relief fund.

"Who would have thought this fund would be so desperately needed?" Keller quipped.

Still, people and businesses already feeling the pain of the pandemic and bristling at government mandates were growing restless. In the first week of April 2020, more than seventy nonessential businesses across Albuquerque were refusing to comply with state public health orders to shut down. Most of those noncompliant businesses were massage parlors and smoke shops, but a few barber shops, beauty salons, and gun stores were also among the scofflaws.

The largest offender in the city was Total Wine and More, which argued that its two Albuquerque stores were essential businesses because they also sold food and therefore could be classified as grocery stores. The state's public health order, however, defined a grocery store as a business devoting at least 50% of its floor space to groceries, and neither Total Wine nor smoke shops that sold a smattering of snacks qualified under that classification.

"A store that sells a few candy bars is not a grocery store," said Gene Gallegos of the City of Albuquerque Fire Marshal's Office.

Businesses committing a first violation received a warning. A citation was issued for a second violation, punishable by a fine of up to $100 or up to six months in jail. Three violations or more and the business was referred to New Mexico State Police, New Mexico Department of Health, or New Mexico Attorney General's Office and socked with a penalty of up to $5,000.

"We're not excited about this," Albuquerque Police Department Lieutenant Sean Wallace said, a grimace spreading across his face during Keller's April 2 news briefing. "We're not trying to come in and take over the city. What we want to do is limit the spread of this virus."

Keller was more to the point.

"You need to be closed today or we are going to close you."

Eventually, Total Wine complied, shutting its doors at both Albuquerque locations after doing a brisk last-minute rush of business on April 7. No citations were issued. By April 8, APD had conducted about 400 business checks for compliance and found that almost all businesses were cooperating.

A few businesses weren't the only ones challenging public health orders in Albuquerque. Impatient golfers were sneaking into shuttered city-operated courses to play a few rounds.

"The city is aware of a few reports of golfers trying to play at Arroyo del Oso," Philip Clelland, the City of Albuquerque Parks and Recreation Department's public information officer, wrote in an email in April 2020, referencing the popular public course. "We have posted signs around all our courses and restricted access to the parking lots. City security will be patrolling the courses and removing any trespassers from the premises."

Albuquerque police had bigger problems to deal with than trespassing golfers and tricky smoke shops. Although overall service calls had decreased by about 2% in the first four months of 2020 compared with the same period in 2019, criminals were still hard at it, adjusting their targets and victims as the pandemic allowed. Auto burglaries and residential burglaries were down since the first weeks of March 2020, likely because more people were staying home, APD Deputy Chief J.J. Griego reported during an April 16 news briefing. Commercial burglaries were up, however, especially among nonessential businesses forced to shut down under public health orders. Domestic violence and hate crimes, especially against Asians because of misplaced blame for the origins of the coronavirus, were also a concern.

Those crime trends were being monitored through APD's Real Time Crime Center and resources were being shifted to address those trends. As a result, detectives from APD's Impact Team and Street Crimes Unit were being shifted over to focus on commercial burglaries as a priority. Detectives, too, were called up to patrol hard-hit areas.

"We're asking officers to be flexible," Keller added. "It's all hands on deck."

Sadly, those hands weren't on deck in time to protect shuttered businesses such as the Anchor + Frame hair salon on Central Avenue in Nob Hill, struck not once but twice by vandals and thieves within a week in April 2020.

The small, airy salon had opened in the fall of 2006, the culmination of nearly thirty years of cutting, coloring, saving money, and dreaming by stylist Gerhardt Ackerman. He remodeled what had been a spin class studio into a cozy showpiece of sleek wood floors, stark white walls, and large plate glass windows to let the sunlight stream through. After being ransacked

The Albuquerque International SunPort's Main Concourse, usually a bustling corridor, a ghost town in April 2020. Photo courtesy Albuquerque Sunport @ ABQSunport on Twitter.

An all but deserted Albuquerque International SunPort passenger pickup and ground transportation area. Photo courtesy Albuquerque Sunport @ABQSunport on Twitter.

twice in 2020, what remained of Anchor + Frame was a hollowed-out hull, its windows and doors broken out and replaced by sheets of particle board, as if the building was girding for a hurricane.

"You Stole It All," Ackerman spray painted across one boarded window. "It's All Gone," he wrote on another. "With restaurants and bars closed, the junkies have free rein on the Central area after 9 p.m. to 8 a.m.," Ackerman said. "There is zero foot traffic or even car traffic."

Mayor Tim Keller and COO Lawrence Rael survey a City of Albuquerque bus as the city battens down health precaution and cleaning measures on public transportation during COVID-19 pandemic. Photo courtesy Mayor's Office, City of Albuquerque.

Albuquerque was largely shut down, per state health orders—an eerie, empty place save for big box stores and COVID-19 testing sites. Gone, too, were the City of Albuquerque's Summerfest concerts through the end of June. The city's big Fourth of July at Balloon Fiesta Park was also likely a no-go.

"This will be a very different summer for all of us," City of Albuquerque COO Lawrence Rael predicted.

The future of the State Fair in September and the Albuquerque International Balloon Fiesta, in October—two of the state's most attended annual events—were also very much up in the air the spring of 2020. Briefly, the Metropolitan Detention Center in downtown Albuquerque also appeared to be shutting itself down after refusing to process certain arrestees it deemed to be COVID-19 risks. Mayor Keller wasn't having it.

"We need our jail to take our prisoners. That's their job," Keller said during an April 16, 2020, news conference, his usually soft and cheery voice replaced with sternness and a slight streak of exasperation. "That's just the way the system works. We've all got to do our part and they've got to do theirs."

That was also Keller's message to the city and its inhabitants, though presented in more encouraging tones: we all have to do our parts. We are in this together. We are one. One Albuquerque.

No amount of cajoling and cheerleading and encouraging, though, could temper the rising tensions felt by some citizens. On April 24, more than one hundred protesters gathered on Marquette Northwest near city hall in downtown Albuquerque, and demanded that Mayor Keller and Governor Lujan Grisham reopen nonessential businesses. The protesters came with American flags and banners and signs, some decrying government tyranny, others making almost comical references to first-world problems, as in "I Want a Haircut!" and "Let My People Golf!" In any other circumstance, those signs would have been taken as jokes, but on that day, no one was laughing. They shouted. They chanted. Drivers circled city hall and made their car horns wail like urban coyotes. Few protesters were social distancing. Fewer were wearing masks. Fewer still had much patience left.

Two days later, on April 26, 2020, Albuquerque City Councilors Brook Bassan and Don Harris announced that they planned to present a resolution to the full council during an upcoming meeting that would call on Mayor Keller to re-evaluate the closing of businesses and facilities under the state's public health orders because of the devastating and unfair effects the closures were having on the local economy.

"Methods such as 20% occupancy levels, wearing masks, and maintaining six-foot social distances should be acceptable to allow our city's small businesses and outdoor facilities to open safely," the councilors said in an email. "Many will be willing to do this, both as businesses and patrons, if it means we can safely restart our local economy."

The resolution ultimately failed 4-5, but it was an indication that even within city government a fissure was already forming. One Albuquerque woman watched the squabbles with growing disdain and immeasurable sadness.

To Shelley Plath, whatever it took to combat the deadly virus was the right thing to do. While she had sympathy for business owners and employees struggling to make a living, she thought they should be grateful to still have lives. She had little sympathy for those who complained that they were being forced to miss playing golf, getting their hair done, shopping at their favorite boutiques, or attending an Isotopes baseball game. That wasn't suffering. That wasn't asking too much to slow the spread of a deadly, unpredictable virus. That all wasn't too much to lose. Shelley Plath missed things far more important than that. She knew how deadly and cruel COVID-19 was because it had ravaged her and the people she loved. Shelley Plath knew what it was like to lose too much.

Shelley was married to Johnny Plath, the son of John Plath, the two men largely responsible for keeping Route 66 aglow with neon. The elder Plath had carried on the work of the neon sign company founded by his father in 1938, opening his own company, Southwest Outdoor Electric, in 1969. When the elder John Plath retired, sons Johnny and Larry took over the business. One of their last projects was the two-year restoration of the refurbished De Anza Motor Lodge sign on Central Avenue east of Nob Hill.

Shelley Plath had not been there January 5, 2020, the night that the De Anza neon sign flickered back to life again under her husband's care and her father-in-law's inspiration. "I thought there might be pictures taken, and I hate having my picture taken," Shelley explained. She had also not been on hand, and neither had any other Plath family member, for the De Anza grand reopening gala in Nob Hill March 2020 when Mayor Keller gave his speech about Albuquerque, a city of crossroads. By then, the Plath family was facing a few crossroads of its own.

"My dad had just died, and I was caring for my ninety-one year-old mother, who was sick and alone, and I was trying to isolate myself from everybody, because I was afraid of getting COVID-19 and infecting her. My father-in-law was also in failing health and hospitalized, but now he was being discharged, and we knew he was not well enough to just go home," Shelley said.

The family decided to place John Plath, the elder—"Pepa" to his eleven grandchildren, eight great-grandchildren and one great-great-grandchild—in Genesis HealthCare's Uptown Rehabilitation Center in Albuquerque. By March 2020, Plath family members had grown concerned about his placement there, because they had heard about what was going on in nursing homes in Washington state and how COVID-19 was spreading through nursing homes and killing many residents, a population especially at risk. Then in early April 2020, two residents and six staffers at the Genesis uptown center in Albuquerque where Pepa was residing tested positive for COVID-19. Weeks later, Genesis became one of the hotspots for COVID-19 deaths. The Plaths knew they needed to bring Pepa home from the center right away. Before they could, the frail ninety-one year-old developed a fever. Out of an abundance of caution, the Plaths asked that Pepa be tested for COVID-19, but their request was denied because his fever had broken on the third day, just before his departure.

Yet without a test, the family could find few home health workers willing to take a risk to care for the elder Plath. Son Johnny Plath decided to move in with Pepa and take over his father's care, aided by his sister and her husband, and one brave home health worker who agreed to come in, test or no test. Had the elder Plath been tested upon leaving the rehab as the family had requested, the test would have come back positive for COVID-19.

On April 8, 2020, five days after his release from the rehab facility, John Plath finally got that COVID-19 test. He died later that same day.

"It was such a cruelty," Shelley Plath said. "We had tried to be so careful. Early on, we were already wearing masks, washing our hands long enough to recite the ABCs, social distancing. But COVID was already inside our homes, and we didn't even know it before it was too late."

Shelley's husband, Johnny Plath, initially tested negative for COVID-19. Even so, he felt sick, and his condition deteriorated quickly. Weeks before, Johnny had been a healthy and active sixty-eight year old, cracking jokes and continuing to work on bringing back to life classic neon signs along Route

The City of Albuquerque's "One Albuquerque" sculpture wears a mask, May 2020. Photo courtesy Mayor's Office, City of Albuquerque.

66. Now he was barely holding on to his life. He got sick so fast that he was rushed to a hospital and placed on a ventilator. After sixteen days in the hospital, Johnny appeared to rally and was taken off the ventilator. Three days later, his condition worsened. A second test confirmed that he was positive for COVID-19. Johnny Plath died a day later, his family left to say goodbye in a video chat. It was May 8, 2020, exactly one month after his father, Pepa, had died.

Johnny Plath's sister and her husband who had also helped care for Pepa tested positive for COVID-19, as did the home health worker, but after varying bouts of illness, they all survived. Another Plath sister tested positive for COVID-19 but pulled through. Brother Larry Plath's wife also became ill with COVID-19, though Larry did not. Her illness left her permanently weakened and unable to work.

"She's what they call a long hauler," Larry said of his wife's experience with COVID-19. "If you're lucky, you survive this thing, but it doesn't always mean survival comes without a lot of consequences."

Shelley Plath and her daughter, Joslyn, also tested positive for COVID-19. They, too, both survived. "I had a fever for two days, body aches, no coughs," Shelley said. "but I never went around my mother again after that."

Shelley couldn't bear to lose anybody else. Because of COVID-19, there was no funeral gathering, no mourning together the family's many losses. Instead, the family held a virtual memorial service for father and son via Zoom. In all, COVID-19 sickened eight members of the Plath family, plus their home health worker. COVID-19 also darkened Southwest Outdoor Electric, ending an eighty-two year family legacy that had brightened the nights in Albuquerque and other destinations along Route 66.

"Heroes Work Here" sign at Lovelace, May 2020. Photo by Roland Penttila, courtesy Albuquerque Museum.

"It was my family history, all that neon, all those signs you see," Larry Plath said. "That was us. That was my family. My grandfather. My father. My brother. All gone."

On the day of Johnny Plath's death, New Mexico officials reported the state had tallied a total of 181 deaths related to COVID-19. The total number of positive cases for COVID-19 was now at 4,673, with 1,030 reported in Bernalillo County.

As May 2020 wore on, those who had clamored for loosening the pandemic restrictions got their wish, at least a little bit. Under revised state public health orders, nonessential businesses could resume sales with curbside pickup and delivery. Golf courses and state parks could open under a number of safety restrictions. Veterinary clinics were back in business. The City of Albuquerque's summer youth program was still a go. Gun stores could welcome back customers by appointment only. By May 16, 2020, all people were required to wear masks when out in public—if they had to be out in public at all.

In Albuquerque, Keller and his team also announced city government's plans to reopen in phases, those plans aligning with the state public health orders.

"It would be easier to stay closed, but we know that's not an option for our city for many reasons," City of Albuquerque CAO Sarita Nair said in a May 14, 2020, email. "Folks just cannot afford to stay home if they are allowed to go back to work. Second, sadly, home is not always safe. We need a place for kids to go where they can be seen and get access to services. And finally, home is not always healthy. We need to have open spaces for people to be in a healthier environment than home might be."

For the first phase of reopening, beginning May 16, 2020, retail stores were allowed to open at 25% capacity, with big box stores remaining at

20%. Churches remained at 10% capacity in May. Parks could reopen. More changes were coming, provided the COVID-19 data remained promising. By May 27, restaurants across the state were being allowed to offer dine-in service through outdoor seating of up to 50% of their outdoor area fire code occupancy.

To help restaurants add al fresco seating, the City of Albuquerque waived permitting and inspection fees for building out patios. In addition, the City of Albuquerque Economic Development Department coordinated with other city departments to provide grants ranging from $2,500 to $10,000 to help the restaurants and other business expand into public sidewalks, parklets, parking lots, and limited street closures. Funding for the grants came from the fed's CARES Act.

New Mexico was also on target to partly open indoor dining at restaurants by June 2020. Hair salons, barber shops, indoor shopping malls, and gyms could possibly also reopen under limitations. The loosening of restrictions was contingent upon how well Albuquerque and the rest of New Mexico did during the Memorial Day weekend at the end of May—how well New Mexicans adhered to the mask

The City of Albuquerque had to communicate changing public messaging around state public health orders, in part through graphics like this one for the mask mandate.

mandate, how much they stayed home, how good they were at refraining from throwing big barbecues, pool parties, and events with others that would have been "normal" before the time of coronavirus.

Just the possibility of reopening began to erase some of the bitterness Gerhardt Ackerman had felt after thieves plundered his Anchor + Frame hair salon in early April. Ackerman's Nob Hill salon was still closed, still boarded up, still hard for him to look at. Yet he was compelled to return to add a new message in spray paint to passersby, even those who did or would do harm to what was left of his dream.

"We love you Nob Hill," Ackerman's message read, "love" symbolized by a large heart. "Stay safe and healthy." He also wrote a note to his customers on his shop's Facebook page: "I just wanted to assure people we will be back when we can. A couple of break-ins and some vandalism won't stop or break me—us."

As Memorial Day weekend neared in 2020, COVID-19 was still taking its toll, slower but surely now in Bernalillo County, which accounted for 1,464 cases out of the 7,624 cases across New Mexico. The state's most populous county— Bernalillo—was no longer the hottest hotspot for virus, though. That dubious and deadly distinction now fell to McKinley County, one of

"George Floyd Sign," May 31, 2020. Photo by Jessica Roybal courtesy Albuquerque Museum, object# PA2021.032.006

Mayor Keller celebrates Del Norte High School graduates during a May 2020 drive-by graduation.

New Mexico's least populated counties, three out of every four of its residents hailing from nearby Navajo, Hopi, and Zuni reservations on the rural western edge of the state. Overall, 351 people had died from COVID-19 and its complications in New Mexico.

On Memorial Day 2020, the death of one man more than 1,400 miles away ignited a season of uprising and a summer of rage that overshadowed even a pernicious pandemic across the country, including in Albuquerque. His death was not a result of COVID-19 but of the virulent discord between law enforcement and people of color, his last painful moments under the knee of a police officer captured on video by a brave teen with a cell phone for all to see. His name was George Floyd.

10

Summer of Rage

For two and a half months, the pandemic paralyzed the country, shocked the system, and exposed the inequality between the haves and the have-nots, who suddenly had even less of nearly everything. The shutdown shredded economic safety nets, revealed disparities in access to healthcare and education, and deepened an already vast political and racial divide. Such inequities hit minorities especially hard, as did the COVID-19 virus, which killed people of color at twice the rate of white Americans.

Then on May 25—Memorial Day 2020—the death of a black man under the knee of a white police officer in Minneapolis shattered the shutdown and led to a national uprising that spilled onto what had largely been emptied streets across America.

The death of George Floyd, whose final gasps and pleas were recorded by a teenage bystander, ignited anger and pain among those who had long been denigrated, mistreated, and disproportionately killed by law enforcement. Just as they had for Breonna Taylor, Philando Castile, Tamir Rice, Michael Brown, Eric Garner, and so many others who had died during encounters with law enforcement, Black Lives Matter movements and other like-minded protesters took to the streets in 2020 holding up banners, posters, and fists to demand that the bloodshed end, that justice prevail, and that minorities and people in the margins stop being used as target practice.

Most of those protests around the country were peaceful. Many protesters wore their masks and social distanced as best they could in a moving crowd, which wasn't much. Along with days and evenings of peaceful protests came nights of violent outbursts. In some places in 2020, city buildings and businesses on fire, police cars burning, looting, broken glass, and tear gas were

Black Lives Matter protestors near UNM in the summer of 2020, photo courtesy of the Mayor's Office, City of Albuquerque.

not uncommon sights. It was as if the cauldron of long simmering fury had finally boiled over. Many considered the blistering combination of poverty, police brutality, and pervasive racism the "other" pandemic, and just as deadly. Among those who watched the video of Floyd die under the knee of Minneapolis police officer Derek Chauvin was Harold Medina, then deputy chief of the Albuquerque Police Department's field services.

"That's just crazy," the thirty-year law enforcement veteran said. "You could see Chauvin just holding him down, and I'm thinking, this is not going to go down well for that police department."

It was a bad maneuver, a needless death, an outrageous breach of protecting and serving, and Medina said he knew it was only a matter of time before the ramifications of what had happened more than 1,400 miles away would hit the streets and the psyches of Albuquerque. He prayed things would stay peaceful.

"People have the right to exercise their First Amendment rights," Medina said. "Our job is to protect them as they do."

Long before George Floyd's death, things had often been tense between APD and the public. New Mexico had ranked in the top three in the nation per capita for deadly shootings by law enforcement officers since 2015, the year the Fatal Force database was created by the *Washington Post*. Many of

Mayor walks with protestors during Black Lives Matter protests, photo courtesy of the Mayor's Office, City of Albuquerque.

New Mexico's shootings were attributed to APD, its bloodiest year coming in 2010 when its officers shot fifteen citizens, nine of them fatally.

Before Minneapolis, APD had been in the national spotlight for deadly use of force after the 2014 slayings of James Boyd, a mentally ill homeless man, his last moments captured on a police body camera, and Mary Hawkes, a nineteen year-old woman running from an armed officer who just happened not to have his body camera turned on in the final moments of her life.

Those shootings and other allegations of excessive use of force caught the attention of the U.S. Department of Justice, which mandated reforms on APD under a court-approved settlement agreement in 2014. APD chafed under the DOJ reforms, but they appeared to work. The rate of officer shootings was declining and tensions were easing, albeit slightly. In 2020, APD had already shot four people, two of them fatally, by the day that George Floyd was killed in Minneapolis.

Harold Medina himself had been involved in two officer shootings years before in Albuquerque. On January 13, 2010, Medina was the ranking officer on the scene at a Northeast Heights 7-Eleven when Kenneth Ellis III, a twenty-five year-old Iraq War veteran with PTSD, put a gun to his own head. Medina aimed his rifle at Ellis as other officers surrounded him. Transcripts in the investigation revealed that Medina was prepared to fire in the split second that Ellis moved his gun from his head, but another officer fired first. The DOJ called the shooting "unreasonable," a failure to de-escalate the situation when a suicidal person was involved. The Ellis family sued APD and the City

Black Lives Matter protest, May 31, 2020, photo by Jessica Roybal, courtesy Albuquerque Museum Digital Archives, object #PA2021.032.005

of Albuquerque for negligence, and a jury awarded the family $10.3 million, one of the largest judgments leveled against APD. The city appealed and later agreed to pay the family $7.95 million. Harold Medina was not named in the lawsuit.

The other shooting was one that burrowed deep into Medina's heart like shrapnel. The death of fourteen year-old Dominic Montoya in September 2002 can still make Medina choke up decades later. The troubled teen—his daughter's classmate, Medina learned later—believed he was tormented by demons when he went to the Taylor Ranch Baptist Church for help after threatening his mother and several neighbors with what appeared to be a pistol, news accounts at the time reported.

Montoya's mother later learned her son had a BB gun, and she and at least three mental health workers who had been treating Montoya called 911 to let officers dispatched to the church know that the gun Dominic had wasn't real. That information never got to the three officers en route. One of the officers was Medina, who had been with APD at that point for seven and a half years.

A church member tried to counsel the teen, praying with Dominic and keeping him calm and distracted so that others in the church could flee to safety. The church member's counseling and prayer appeared to work. Montoya was leaving the church and was inside the foyer when officers arrived and ordered him to stop and show his hands. In a split second, the teen turned his back to the officers then spun around with the gun in his hand and pointed it at them. One officer dove for cover. Harold Medina fired three times, striking the teen twice in the abdomen. Dominic Montoya was pronounced dead at the hospital.

Churchgoers reported that Medina appeared shaken by the shooting, so they prayed with and for him. As traumatic as that shooting was, Medina said it helped make him a better, more compassionate leader, willing to examine both sides of an issue, especially those involving lethal use of force.

"I'll always live with that," Medina said of Montoya's death in a 2020 interview with the *Albuquerque Journal*.

"These are tragedies that a community lives with forever, and that's why we have to do everything we can to make sure that we're developing policies and procedures which lessen our likelihood of these incidents occurring."

On May 28, 2020, a Thursday, and three days after George Floyd's death, an estimated 400 protesters marched peacefully up and down Central Avenue in Albuquerque, chanting and carrying signs that read "No lives matter until Black Lives Matter," "Say his name," and "No justice, no peace."

The protest began at 6 p.m. at Wyoming and Central Southeast on the eastern edge of the International District, an ethnically rich community with a lengthy and uneasy history with law enforcement. By 10 p.m., the protest was winding down. Cars that had earlier filled the Teriyaki Chicken Bowl parking lot on the northeast corner of the intersection were nearly all gone.

Command of the officers on the ground was, as always, handled by a lieutenant, and on that night it was Lieutenant John Pierson*, a fifteen-year veteran at APD, watching from the city's Real Time Crime Center, where consoles, computers, and sixteen television screens monitor the goings on in Albuquerque's streets and neighborhoods. The highly restricted center is nicknamed "The Bridge," as in the main command and control facility of a starship in Star Trek, and besides the small staff that monitors and analyzes incoming data, only the lieutenant in charge is allowed inside. Even APD top brass, Mayor Keller, and CAO Sarita Nair, whose responsibilities include APD, are relegated to a separate room.

"We do that to minimize the noise," Lieutenant Pierson said, "noise" being a nice way to refer to any meddling or second-guessing by the other officials.

That Thursday evening, May 28, 2020, officers had served as traffic control, shutting down parts of Central as the protesters made their way up and down the street. Several blocks away, a contingent of Emergency Response Team officers clad in ominous black riot gear sat in city buses, prepared to jump into action should things go sideways. Also tucked away was a BearCat, an armored tactical vehicle.

"It's what we do when we expect large crowds," Medina said. "But you don't see them unless we need them."

On the night of May 28, 2020, it appeared these contingencies weren't needed. Lieutenant Pierson was ready to call it a night and send his officers home around 10 p.m. when a crowd of about thirty people meandering about the McDonald's parking lot on the northwest corner of Central and Wyoming began causing trouble. This crowd was different, he thought. This crowd had a different temperature.

"It seemed like they came out of nowhere and had a different agenda," Pierson said. "An after-hours crowd with a different mentality."

Pierson was aware that the stragglers were tagging nearby bus stops with spray paint and vandalizing parked cars. A traffic sergeant preparing to leave the scene was momentarily trapped in her vehicle as about twenty people surrounded her, kicking and pummeling her vehicle, and busting a window until she was able to break free from the taunting scrum. Maybe, Pierson thought, these people were just tired of being cooped up at home during COVID and blowing off steam. Maybe, with bars and nightclubs closed, this was something for them to do. Something not good.

Pierson weighed whether to send in the Emergency Response Team or field officers to break up the crowd, but he was concerned that an increased police presence could blow up the situation. Rules of engagement were based on the level of property devastation, and this situation had not risen to that level.

*The source's name has been changed to protect his identity.

Then came reports of a "39-3," code for shots fired, around 11 p.m. near the McDonald's. The shots were also picked up by APD's new ShotSpotter, a gunshot detection system that alerts law enforcement to when and where a gun has been fired by measuring the distance from dozens of sound sensors around the city. The alert is then transmitted to a hub in California to confirm whether the sound was from a firearm or some other source such as fireworks. Then the information is sent to dispatchers, The Bridge at APD's Real Time Crime Center, and to officers through a cell phone app, all in a matter of seconds.

In all, thirty-three shots were detected around the McDonald's that night. Reports on the ground indicated that the shots were being fired by at least one vehicle. At different times, the shooters' vehicle was reported as a Buick, Kia, or Jaguar.

Pierson called in air support, so he could get a bird's eye view of the situation. The APD chopper circled overhead in the area, transmitting grainy black and white night vision footage of the scene and targeting a silver four-door Kia looping slowly around McDonald's, into its parking lot, onto nearby streets, then back again. From the air, four passengers were visible inside, their ghostly white visages atop arms and bodies poking out of a passenger window and an open sunroof. The crowd was growing now, maybe fifty or seventy strong. The Kia made another round of the McDonald's. More shots were fired. It was time to move in, but slowly, patiently, and away from the crowd.

The Kia traveled west on Central as unmarked police cars followed at a short distance. When the Kia reached thirteen blocks, officers made the traffic stop, lights and sirens on, bunching behind the Kia as it pulled onto Mesilla Southeast, the fourteenth block. Officers, their firearms locked on the vehicle, slowly approached, shouting directives for its four occupants to toss the keys in the street and exit one by one, hands up. The driver's door opened and out bolted a young man, ignoring police commands as he ran north, scrambling over fences and stumbling through an auto repair lot and backyards, all the while under the watchful eyes of air support and Pierson.

Officers were advised to form a perimeter and hold steady while two SWAT teams organized a search. But the search was over before it began. After three minutes, the absconder surrendered, emerging from a yard at the end of the block, raising his hands in the air and walking back toward the awaiting officers and his three cohorts, now lying facedown in the street.

"I was just trying to see what was going on here," one of the young men shouted. "What the fuck." In police body camera footage, officers referred to him as the "little mouth one" because he wouldn't stop talking, even though an officer repeatedly asked him to "chill."

Officers began processing the scene and discussed who would transport the four teens, identified as the eighteen year-old Hispanic driver, his sixteen year-old "little mouth" brother, and two African-American friends, but they had company.

Several of the after-hours crowd from McDonald's had found their way to Mesilla Street, and they were angry. Though it's unclear how, one person in the group said they showed up after hearing that police were holding guns to the heads of four young African-American men. That wasn't true, but it didn't matter. To this crowd, no matter what the police were doing, it had to be bad.

"Children! You're trying to kill our children!" one woman shouted.

"Do not talk to them. Stop fucking talking," another shouted at the mouthy brother. "You haven't read him his rights. Shut the fuck up. Fuck the police. Don't even talk to me unless you read me my rights. You going to school me, fucking pig?"

More onlookers kept coming, shouting, screaming, some holding their hands in the air as if they were surrendering. "Respect the people!" they shouted. "We got rights!" "Go back to China if you're going to be like this!" "We are fighting for justice! You motherfuckers are on the wrong side!" "What the fuck is wrong with you?"

An officer radioed dispatch: "We need more units down here. Now."

Two young women, apparently more observers than agitators, walked up to one officer and asked him what it was like to be a police officer and see a peaceful protest end in such acrimony, especially so soon after George Floyd.

"It's unfortunate," the officer replied.

Harold Medina was now at the Bridge. Both he and Lieutenant Pierson—and, likely, every other officer on scene—knew that it was time to go.

"Drive the car to the sub(station) and everybody else clears ASAP," came the order over the police radio.

"As soon as we get into that car and try to drive it away there's going to be a confrontation," came the response.

"You're going to have a big-ass riot now," the mouthy brother said. He might have been right.

APD's BearCat rolled in, preparing to scoop up the four teens and carry them away from the confrontation. Dozens of members of the Emergency Response Team moved in from the north, forming a fortified line facing the protesters but from a distance. The idea was for the riot-clad team to distract the crowd as the other officers departed in their vehicles, many now with their windows bashed in, broken glass sparkling in the streetlights of East Central.

The distraction worked. The officers left. The BearCat rolled in. Left behind was the Kia, its keys on the car roof, and with it any evidence that may have tied the teens to at least some of the shots fired. Even if there had been weapons and ammo in the car, they would likely not be admissible at trial since the possession of the evidence, the chain of custody, had been broken. Despite APD's attempt to temper its moves, the BearCat, the riot-clad officers, the military-grade weapons, and the helicopter whirling overhead had sent a message to the protesters that they were under attack.

"You going to hurt us with those fucking batons?" one protester shouted. "Nobody has a weapon. How can we hurt you guys?"

Another protester yelled, "We all just waiting for you guys to violate our constitutional rights."

Still another predicted, "I can't wait to see you shoot that thing. I'll have your job, boy."

Lapel camera footage from several ERT members as well as video livestreamed from protesters' cell phones documented the confrontation, each side seeing something different than the other.

"They showed up on us in the darkness," one protester said. "It was fifty community members being attacked by three buses of riot cops." But the ERT officers had never gotten close to the community members, video showed.

The confrontation lasted about thirty minutes, the protesters growing more impatient, their words angrier. The officers remained silent as protesters called them racist, dumbasses, communists, child haters, God haters, and Nazis. The team was given the command: as soon as air support flooded the area with its bright spotlights, officers were supposed to quickly retreat to the buses.

"If we're attacked, will there be support?" one officer asked.

"If they start 27-4ing you, handle appropriately," was the response, "27-4" being police code for assault and battery.

"I think we should throw smoke," one officer suggested. "They're going to follow us."

"That might instigate more," another countered.

In the end, at least three tear gas canisters were tossed to create a barrier of stinging smoke to stop the protesters from reaching the buses. Body camera footage appears to show that the canisters were thrown some distance in front of the protesters. Still, a woman in the crowd was apparently struck with one. It was unclear whether she had been closer to the retreating officers than the others, or whether the canister that struck her was picked up by another protester and hurled at the fleeing officers and hit her instead. On the police scanner, the woman's injury was reported as minor, not requiring medical attention.

"It was a hairy exit," one officer said.

"We're good," Lieutenant Pierson told APD officers. "Good job."

At a news conference the next day, both Mayor Keller and then APD chief Michael Geier defended APD for showing restraint and handling the situation well.

"Dozens of shots were fired and APD absolutely had to respond," Mayor Keller said. "They did it in a way that fortunately kept everyone safe, and while I know it was scary for many, it was also dangerous for many."

Shortly after the city presser, a group of protesters who had been at the scene of the protest held a news conference of their own to refute the city's assessment, saying that police had earlier allowed a man in a truck to try to run down some of the protesters at the McDonald's. Protesters contended that APD had racially profiled the teens in the Kia, had not read them their rights, had stolen their property, and had callously left their car in the street.

Protesters questioned why so many heavily armed officers had to take down the teens, why they had to call in riot cops and tanks, and why that sort of intense presence was used against predominantly minority protesters in the minority-heavy International District. Nothing of the sort was used at a protest held in April against COVID-19 shutdown orders in which a majority of the participants were white.

"There was the perception, regardless of what APD did or didn't try to do, the strong perception, that APD was coming down hard on protesters and black and brown people," said Michelle Melendez, director of the City of Albuquerque Office of Equity and Inclusion. "APD's actions weren't helpful in the way it perceived them to be."

Both Mayor Keller and Harold Medina at APD knew there were lessons to be learned as to how the city handled the night of May 28, 2020. Other cities were experiencing daily protests and nightly violence, presumably led by different factions, and there was no reason not to believe that the same wouldn't happen in Albuquerque. Melendez would be crucial in helping law enforcement learn those lessons.

"We didn't have a lot of protocols that night," Mayor Keller said. "We as a city had not had much experience of late with any tense protests. We had experienced protests like the Women's March and March for Our Lives, political rallies and protests involving immigrant detainees, but nothing like that since I have been in office."

Medina started looking more intently at how other police forces in other cities were handling their protests and mass gatherings in 2020, and what he learned was that the events that became quickly inflamed were those situations where police took over as the focal point.

"When you had your officers out in riot gear, and they could just be in line standing there, that exacerbated the crowd," Medina observed. "When police marched with the protesters, it was a different outcome."

There had to be a balance between police being there to protect and police being there, even inadvertently, to incite. That balance would be put to the test again in Albuquerque three nights after the McDonald's melee. Once again, not everybody would agree with how well the city and APD handled it all.

On the evening of May 31, 2020, the Albuquerque Center for Peace and Justice sponsored a candlelight vigil to honor the memory of George Floyd outside its offices on Harvard Drive, two blocks south of Central Avenue near the University of New Mexico. Thousands of people of all colors and ages, most wearing masks, stood holding signs and using their cell phone lights as candles as they sang Amazing Grace and listened to speakers, among them Mayor Keller. As Keller spoke, some in the crowd yelled "Defund the police! Defund the police!" Keller could feel that in the mix of peace and unity was frustration and anger.

"It was palpable," Keller said. "I was thinking all that emotion is going to go somewhere, and a candlelight vigil and prayer wasn't going to cut it."

Still, the crowd remained peaceful as it poured out onto Central Avenue, the vigil turning to march downtown and back up through the university area and east toward Nob Hill. Police noted a few agitators in the crowd, a few broken windows, a dumpster fire near Lead and Harvard Southeast.

"All in all, we felt positive about it," Keller said. "APD was prepared, and they were working to protect the protesters by shutting down the street as they marched. We saw how other cities were on fire because they were sending out riots cops from the start. We felt we were handling things better."

Harold Medina situated himself at his command post. APD had eyes everywhere—on rooftops, in the air, in the crowds, undercover. Things were going well. Around 10 p.m., the crowds thinned. Officers noted that vehicles driven by attendees were heading out. Everyone was clearing. APD officers, including the Emergency Response Team that had been on call again, ready but hidden from view, were told to stand down and go home.

"Thanks for your work tonight," came a voice on police radios. "You guys are great."

Medina heaved a sigh of relief, got in his truck, and headed home. About midnight, as he was in bed asleep, or nearly so, his phone rang. It was his son.

"Dad, are you seeing what's going on downtown? You need to find out what's going on."

Medina called Chief Geier. He called dispatchers with APD's Valley Command, which oversees downtown. Things were rapidly spiraling out of control. Downtown was under attack. Medina headed out.

Mayor Keller was finishing up email correspondence and about to get ready for bed when he was called about the situation downtown. Things are changing, he heard. It was bad.

"I said a couple of prayers," Keller said "then started waking up everybody on the civilian side."

It was as if the rioters were tuned in to police scanners and knew to move in after officers had been told to stand down and go home. It was as if they wanted to make it appear that the mayhem was a continuation of the earlier peaceful protest. These were not the protesters. These were not Black Lives Matter groups. These were agitators and instigators and those who simply saw an opportunity to go crazy, and about eighty to one hundred of them were running wild all over downtown Albuquerque. Earlier in the day, police had been made aware of social media chatter indicating that outsiders were being asked to come to Albuquerque to cause trouble. When those first calls came in that night, Keller wondered if this was what that social media chatter was about.

Rioters were smashing storefront windows, spray painting graffiti on anything with a surface, and setting fires in dumpsters and trashcans. Several rioters broke the windows of a restaurant at Third and Central, pulled out the restaurant's chairs, and situated them around a blaze in the middle of the intersection, where they chugged bottles of alcohol looted from nearby bars, as if hanging out around a campfire. Motorcycles and cars, many with passengers dangling outside and hollering, raced through the streets. Security alarms wailed. Rioters tossed bar glasses in the air, sending shards everywhere as they shattered on the pavement. They sprayed fire extinguishers in plumes of gas and powder like mini geysers.

The marauders had a head start on police, but not for long. Police and riot-clad ERT officers massed along the edge of downtown. Loudspeakers from APD's helicopter circling above issued commands for the people below to leave the area. Rioters taunted the officers, yelling obscenities similar to those spewed a few nights before. Someone threw what appeared to be a flaming Molotov cocktail toward the officers.

"It was unreal," Harold Medina said. "I've never seen anything like it."

The pivotal moment came as rioters began to swarm the venerated KiMo Theatre at Fifth and Central. They set fires in front of and behind the historic building. They broke windows and doors and made their way inside, several climbing to the rooftop, where what was believed to be gunshots were fired at officers. It seemed only a matter of time before they would set fires inside, if they hadn't already. Medina feared that the more than ninety year-old building was in grave peril. Things had gone way too far.

"We're not going to let them get the KiMo," he said.

It was too dangerous to send officers inside the theater, especially if there were people with guns lying in wait. The command was made to roll in the BearCat close to the front of the theater and let loose a barrage of tear gas inside to flush out the infiltrators. It worked.

"Everybody ran out," Medina said. "It was like a moral victory to save the KiMo."

Then APD had to save the rest of downtown. Two columns of police in riot gear, one at Second and Central and the other at Third and Central, moved in, raising batons in front of them and stepping together, pushing back the crowd physically and, later, with tear gas and rubber bullets.

Before dawn, the siege was finally over. Medina walked through the streets, the crunch of broken glass under his feet. Trash was everywhere. Hateful slogans were splashed in paint along the walls. The pungent odor of tear gas mixed with the charred and choking smell of smoke from at least thirty-three fires set in the area filled the air. Medina thanked the officers slumped on the sidewalks, bone tired, their faces drenched in sweat, their eyes blinking back disbelief.

"One of my biggest regrets was that I didn't have water to bring them," Medina recalled. "I saw how thirsty they were, how tired they were. I saw how hard they had worked." He walked toward the SWAT officers outside the KiMo Theater, which they had saved hours before. The officers refused to let Medina shake their hands or hug them.

"Chief," they told him, "you shouldn't touch us. We have too much tear gas still on us."

Then Deputy Chief Harold Medina meets downtown with business owners the morning after violence erupted in Albuquerque.

Medina drove to his Westside home and sat in his driveway for at least ten minutes, thinking about how proud he was of these officers—and how bad he felt for them.

"I knew there would be criticism about how we handled things," he said. "I knew we had a long way to go before any of this was better." Medina was especially worried about the younger cops coming on the force at a time when their profession was so maligned, sometimes rightly so, but most times not. "We older senior officers knew a different time. In my career, everybody loved the cops."

In the aftermath, downtown Albuquerque reflected what so many other cities were experiencing night after night, but fortunately, unlike other cities, no lives had been claimed.

Mayor Keller meets with workers in front of boarded up windows downtown.
Photo courtesy of the Mayor's Office, City of Albuquerque.

Mayor Keller hadn't slept yet. He was already at work, trying to find the right words to calm his city. He and COO Lawrence Rael went downtown at dawn to offer encouragement to the people who were hard at work, cleaning up the aftermath. He made sure his team was already doing what needed to be done downtown and looking ahead toward what came next. It was June 1, 2020, the day New Mexico's restaurants, gyms, salons, and malls were allowed to reopen at partial capacity under Governor Lujan Grisham's eased COVID-19 public health orders. Reopening would have to wait for some of the businesses downtown, though. Workers with the Solid Waste Department cleaned up what could be cleaned up. The city's planning department oversaw the installation of plywood over broken windows.

"We paid for that and offered to pay for the glass, but many businesses didn't want that until after the COVID-19 shutdown," Keller said.

Bree Ortiz scrolled through social media that morning, searching for information on how badly damaged the city was. As the division manager for community events, part of the City of Albuquerque Arts & Culture Department, Ortiz was especially worried about the KiMo, one of the venues her department oversees.

"I had this sick feeling, the dread of what was going to be left," Ortiz said. "It was so surreal, like a horror movie." Her phone rang just after 6 a.m. Dr. Shelle Sanchez, Director of Arts & Culture, and several staff members were already at the KiMo.

Paint for Peace artwork at the KiMo, July 11, 2020, photo by Bobby Gutierrez, courtesy of the Albuquerque Museum Digital Archives, object #PA2021.033.015

"Is it still standing?" Ortiz asked nervously.

"Yes, it's still standing," Sanchez replied.

Larry Parker, longtime manager of the KiMo, had slept through it all, unaware that his beloved venue had nearly been destroyed. Joe Anderson, owner of the Launchpad, a nightclub two blocks west of the KiMo on Central Avenue, had texted Parker a photo of the overnight melee, but Parker had not seen it until he was up and preparing for his next day. Because the pandemic shutdown had canceled all events at the KiMo, Parker had been transferred to the city's Emergency Operations Center to help coordinate the COVID wellness hotel program. When Parker saw Anderson's photo of the KiMo doors kicked in and the windows shattered, he knew where he had to go.

"Holy fuck," Parker said to his wife. "I'm out of here."

In all, eight large windows and three glass doors had to be replaced at the KiMo, costing the city an estimated $10,000 to $12,000. It was the fourth time windows had been broken that fiscal year. Repairs to the interior of the theater, including fumigating the building of tear gas and smoke, also had to be done. Ticket scanners, the only items stolen, could be replaced.

Two months before the riotous night downtown, the city's then Cultural Services Department (now Department of Arts & Culture) had applied to Albuquerque's Landmarks and Urban Conservation Commission for security shutters to be placed over all windows and doors of the KiMo. Because the building is designated as a registered historic landmark, renovations such as the shutters have to maintain the architectural significance of the theater and be approved by both the landmark commission and the New Mexico Historic Preservation Division at the state level. Approvals would take time. Until then, plywood would be the face of the KiMo. At least it was still standing.

Black Lives Matter chalk mural on Civic Plaza in Albuquerque. Photo courtesy of the Mayor's Office, City of Albuquerque.

Paint for Peace window art at 4th and Central, summer 2020, photo courtesy of the Mayor's Office, City of Albuquerque

Just as Medina had expected, criticism came quickly as to how APD handled the incident. The *Albuquerque Journal* chided Mayor Keller for failing to improve downtown as he had promised, even before the riots. The editorial board chided APD for intervening in the melee late. It called for Keller to impose a city curfew at sundown and to bring in the National Guard to keep the peace.

Black Lives Matter chalk mural on City of Albuquerque's Civic Plaza. Photo courtesy of the Mayor's Office, City of Albuquerque.

"The level of violence nationwide appears to be increasing daily as peaceful protests are tarnished by those hellbent on destruction," the *Journal* editorial read. "That was the case in Albuquerque."

Mayor Keller said no to the suggestions. Like Medina, he believed that a wide berth of tolerance should to be given to allow protesters to exercise their right to free speech. Police had their role to play, but it was not to crush, inflame, or step in until it was necessary to protect the public. Keller still believed in Albuquerque and its ability to come together in the worst of times. Keller and city leaders also recognized the stark differences between what happened on that single night downtown in contrast to the weeks on end of riots, destruction and even death in places like Portland, Los Angeles, and Minneapolis. The gaping difference in outcomes is attributed to restraint.

"What we saw overnight downtown was not a protest, and it was not Albuquerque," Keller wrote in a statement to the city that afternoon. "Protesting is our constitutional right as Americans. We are strongest when we use it to come together as one and use our voices to express outrage and call for change, rather than using our hands to tear each other down."

Outside the KiMo Theatre, boarded up and vacant, the marquee read, "WE'RE ALL IN THIS TOGETHER."

Two weeks later, Albuquerque once again faced violence in the streets, raising questions again about how the city and its police handled unfolding events. Racial tensions again erupted, and some again wondered how "together" the city really was.

Black Lives Matter protestors walk in downtown Albuquerque in the summer of 2020. Photo courtesy of the Mayor's Office, City of Albuquerque.

Mayor Keller joins a prayer at the One Albuquerque sculpture. Photo courtesy of the Mayor's Office, City of Albuquerque.

Kids hold signs supporting Black Lives Matter in downtown Albuquerque. Photo courtesy of the Mayor's Office, City of Albuquerque.

Protesters climbing the City of Albuquerque's One Albuquerque sculpture, which is also donning a mask. Photo courtesy of the Mayor's Office, City of Albuquerque.

Mayor Keller walks with protesters at one of the many peaceful marches in Albuquerque in June 2020. Photo courtesy of the Mayor's Office, City of Albuquerque.

*The history of New Mexico is steeped in
controversy, complexity, brutality and
blood, and that which our ancestors did or
didn't do should be seen within the prism
of its time, or so historians tell us.*

11

Oñate

Michelle Melendez was made for handling pandemics. Her experience includes years of working in various capacities for the New Mexico Department of Health, serving as director of EleValle Community Health Collaborative in Albuquerque's South Valley, and holding leadership roles for both First Choice Community Healthcare and CHI St. Joseph's Children health services. Melendez also served on several health and education boards and was a reporter for the *Albuquerque Journal*. Most importantly, she grew up in Albuquerque and knows its people, knows its strengths and its weaknesses, its heartbeat and its heartaches, and its culture and its diversity. She knows Albuquerque's most vulnerable populations—its refugees, its homeless, its minorities, and its impoverished—and she cares about them.

Mayor Tim Keller knew Michelle Melendez was someone he needed in his administration when he chose her in March 2018 to lead the City of Albuquerque Office of Equity and Inclusion, an expanded and revitalized version of what had been the city's Office of Diversity and Human Rights.

"He had an idea and he hired me on the spot," said Melendez, an intense woman who readily calls out bullshit and passionately pinpoints problems and solutions.

Melendez met Keller when he was a New Mexico state senator representing the low-income, ethnically diverse and struggling neighborhoods off East Central Avenue that had earned the dubious nickname the "War Zone" because of the near-nightly sounds of gunfire, the wail of police sirens, the danger, and the fear.

"I took him on walking tours of the neighborhoods," Melendez said of Mayor Keller. "He really wanted to know the communities, who the people are, and what they needed from him." She and other residents in the area, including longtime community activist Reynaluz Juarez, helped him see the need to reframe the area as the International District. Juarez and Mayor Keller were advocates for the public library that was built on East Central, a space hoped to enhance community in the International District and another major construction project pushed through during COVID-19. Melendez said Keller impressed her with his desire to help Albuquerque live up to its potential as a city of equality and inclusiveness. Melendez had impressed him as the one to help in that effort.

"We want to make true what we say we are," Melendez said. "My staff's job is how can we help every city department do better—who we do business with, where we are investing, how we are providing services, and how we make services more accessible." Then came COVID-19.

Melendez immediately volunteered to wear many hats aside from her directorial one. She stepped up to take a leadership role as the leader of City Operations, one of four divisions of responsibility that also included planning, finance, and logistics. Operations, as the name implies, oversees housing, food, mass care, medical services, and seemingly every other aspect that was tied to the city's response to COVID-19. Ask anybody who sought assistance from the city during the pandemic, and chances are it was Michelle Melendez who served as their contact, able to make things happen as needed. But after the George Floyd killing and with civil unrest growing, it was time for Director Melendez to get back to the job she was hired to do in the Office of Equity and Inclusion.

Melendez had questions for APD, particularly Harold Medina, then deputy chief. She pointed out that APD brass were blind to the way many residents in the community viewed the police.

"It was important for them to understand that police not hitting a protester in the head with a baton or not beating people did not mean that people perceived them as being their protectors," she said. "They still used tear gas, rubber bullets," said Melendez of APD. "They called armed white militia people 'armed friendlies.' None of that was helpful."

Melendez was there to ask the uncomfortable questions. She attended or monitored most, if not all of the protests in Albuquerque in 2020, rallies and vigils organized by those associated with the Black Lives Matter movement, and gatherings of indigenous and civil rights groups. There were plenty of public events for activists that year—an estimated fifty protests in Albuquerque over the course of the summer alone. Since that first protest on May 28, 2020, near Wyoming and Central, which led to a heated confrontation, a protest seemed to occur every day that summer—the vast majority of them peaceful, productive, and largely ignored by the media.

"Offers were made by APD to the protest groups as to whether they wanted security and traffic control," Melendez said. "Some did. Some had their own security. Some didn't need traffic control." Some protesters, she said, didn't believe that APD would protect them.

La Jornada by Reynaldo Rivera and Betty Sabo, statue outside on the corner of the Albuquerque Museum grounds. Photo courtesy of Albuquerque Museum.

Still, the initial decisions police made that summer had served as hard lessons, and Medina and his lieutenants appeared to be willing students on how to improve matters. She noted that officers were learning how to hold back better, how to be there only as needed, and how to avoid intimidating or inciting protesters. While de-escalation was an improvement, on June 15, 2020, as people gathered around the controversial statue of Don Juan de Oñate at the Albuquerque Museum, it felt as if police had gone too far in the direction of passivity.

The history of New Mexico is steeped in controversy, complexity, brutality and blood, and that which our ancestors did or didn't do should be seen within the prism of its time, or so historians tell us. The Spanish settlements from which many New Mexican families derive their ancestry began in the 1590s when Don Juan de Oñate led a group of settlers, missionaries, and livestock to the crossroads of New Mexico and staked claim to the land for Spain. With Oñate came Hispanic culture, civilization, new crops, and Christianity, which gave root to the way many modern day New Mexicans live their lives. To them, Oñate is the forefather of New Mexico and "native" New Mexicans.

Protesters and Curandera at the Oñate protest. Photo courtesy Lonnie J. Anderson.

Numbe Whageh land sculpture, by Naranjo Morse, at the Albuquerque Museum. Photo courtesy Albuquerque Museum.

La Jornada statue detail of Millie Santillanes, by Betty Sabo. Photo courtesy of Albuquerque Museum.

Oñate was the man of the hour as New Mexico planned to commemorate its Cuarto Centenario, the 400th anniversary of the arrival of Spanish colonists, in 1998. In Albuquerque, the fire behind those efforts was Millie Santillanes, a small woman with a big personality who had served in city government, in Old Town business, and as an advocate for honoring Hispanic culture. Santillanes often referred to herself as just a "five-foot, 200-pound grandma." Others called her "La Jefa," the boss.

Santillanes had begun lobbying for a statue, perhaps a bust, to honor Oñate several years before 1998. As months passed and word spread of the statue, so did controversy. Oñate, who became New Mexico's first colonial governor, was not always gracious to those who were already here when he arrived. At times, he was downright ruthless to the Native Americans who had long called this land their home. An ambush at Acoma that left several Spaniards dead, including Oñate's nephew, led to a massive retaliation against the Pueblo inhabitants. Oñate ordered his men to kill hundreds of them, forcing the rest into servitude and calling for the right foot of each adult male to be severed. For those barbarous acts, Oñate was removed from power and banished from New Mexico. That violent episode became Oñate's bloody legacy.

None of these dubious details dissuaded Santillanes, who questioned and dismissed some of the details in the Acoma story. Millie Santillanes believed that Don Juan de Oñate should be revered—not reviled—controversy or not.

"Art is, in and of itself, controversial," Santillanes often said. "It's designed to stimulate discussion."

Months of often heated discussion between city councilors, arts boards, historians, and the public eventually led to the uneasy decision to install a much larger piece of Oñate at Mountain and 19th Northwest, outside the Albuquerque Museum near Tiguex Park, in the hopes of providing not only context to the role Oñate played in the state's history but also a sense of multicultural unity.

Renowned artists Betty Sabo, Reynaldo "Sonny" Rivera, and Nora Naranjo Morse were commissioned to create the artwork. Their pieces were completed too late for the 1998 Cuarto Centenario celebration, was at least five times more expensive than the original estimated cost of $100,000, and was so polarizing that for a time not even the artists could agree on what it should look like. Eventually, the creative team decided on two works of art, designed to complement and contrast each other. Rivera and Sabo created the massive, more well-known piece, *La Jornada*, which features thirty-three life-size bronze figures of Spanish settlers, conquistadors, missionaries, children, and livestock led by Oñate as they make their way over the high desert's parched and rocky terrain.

"It is magnificent," Santillanes said when shown a model of the proposed work in 1999. "We would be the pride of the Southwest with this memorial."

Artist Naranjo Morse's piece, *Numbe Whageh*, meaning "the center place," uses natural elements of earth, water, and native vegetation to express the Native American connection to the environment. A path spirals deeper into the earth to the center place. A reflecting pool below sidewalk level at the museum, far beneath the rocky berm where the bronzes of Oñate and the settlers reside, catches reflections cast by the caravan above. As one emerges from the shaded center of Morse's piece, the settlers come into greater view. Naranjo Morse, a member of Santa Clara Pueblo, has said her piece captures her ancestors' natural, serene home and envisions what they must have seen when settlers arrived.

La Jornada statue detail of former City of Albuquerque Director of Cultural Services, Millie Santillanes, by Betty Sabo. Photo courtesy of Albuquerque Museum.

La Jornada was finally installed in 2005. Onlookers that day reported seeing Millie Santillanes there with a smile on her face and a tear in her eye. One of the figures in the sculpture—that of a short, smiling woman with her head covered in a traditional rebozo, reaching out to a child—was created by Betty Sabo in Santillanes' likeness to honor her efforts to bring the monument to fruition.

"Al fin," Santillanes said as she beheld *La Jornada*. Finally.

Millie Santillanes died two years later at age seventy-four, but the controversy that surrounded the Oñate artwork and *La Jornada* was anything but final with her death.

The death of George Floyd in May 2020, renewed a reconsideration of American monuments, flags, symbols, and holidays. Dozens of statues of Confederate icons, viewed as emblems of slavery and racism, came down across the country. Mississippi announced it was redesigning its state flag to eliminate the patch of Confederate battle flag in the corner. A handful of states, including New Mexico, now celebrated the second Monday in October as Indigenous Peoples' Day, kicking Christopher Columbus to the curb. Some called it erasing history; others called it exposing the darker part of history, unworthy of revisionist whitewashing and praise.

In Albuquerque, the movement toward racial justice once again renewed the conflict over Oñate and his bloody legacy against Pueblo Indians. In a letter dated June 11, 2020, the Albuquerque Museum's board of trustees asked Mayor Keller to have *La Jornada* removed from its location on museum grounds, saying the sculpture "has caused conflict, pain, and has divided our communities" since its inception. Keller responded the next day in a written statement announcing that he would ask the city's public arts board to make a recommendation on *La Jornada*.

"This is not the first time our city has had a deep conversation about this statue, and it's time we have it again," Mayor Keller wrote in his response.

Three days later, the conversation about *La Jornada* was forced, beginning peacefully when a group called Genizaro Nation organized a prayer gathering on June 15 at Tiguex Park, across the street from the museum and the statue. Genizaro Nation, whose name derives from enslaved Native Americans who eventually assimilated into the Hispanic families that had held them captive, called for the removal of the Oñate statue because of the trauma and the treachery he imposed on native people.

That night, APD's Lieutenant John Pierson* was the incident commander again. He settled in for the duration at the Real Time Crime Center. His event action plan called for two Emergency Response Teams and other APD personnel to be on hand but out of sight, one group tucked away inside the Albuquerque Museum and another group several blocks away.

"The Department recognizes that in order to avoid unnecessary confrontation with protesters it must display some discretion in the application of the law," Pierson wrote in the plan. If his officers were needed to protect lives and prevent major property damage, they could be on the scene within seconds. If they weren't, then it was another easy night.

"We saw a lot of other cities that had large-scale protests, and Chief Medina noticed that any protest where the initial response was to send in riot officers always escalated quickly," Pierson said. The APD plan called for protecting the museum and the historically valuable items inside, much as police had protected the KiMo Theatre during the June 1 riot. The Oñate statue was another matter.

"I wasn't worried about the statue," Lieutenant Pierson said. "It was secured in ten feet of concrete. There was no way it was going to be brought down, so it wasn't a big concern. They could tie a chain around it and try to pull it down with a truck, but it wasn't going to move."

Some folks in the crowd that night were still willing to try. People, some in native dress, beat drums, chanted, and burned sage as they gathered on the rocky berm where the Oñate statue was affixed. Speakers talked about their solidarity with Black Lives Matter movements and their opposition to white supremacy. They vowed to convince city officials to take down Oñate, once and for all.

Nearby, several dozen protesters were not satisfied with songs and smudging sage. They began shouting "Tear it down! Tear it down!" Someone attached a sign to the statue that read "Oñate No Vale Verga," a vulgarity involving male genitalia. Someone wrapped a chain around the statue. Another used a pickaxe to try to damage the resilient bronze.

A different group brought items far more lethal—assault-style rifles and lots of them. Some at the scene may have recognized the heavily armed khaki- and camo-clad interlopers as members of the New Mexico Civil Guard, a militia group that had recently shown up at peaceful Black Lives Matter protests, supposedly to protect property and Albuquerque citizens, but serving mostly to intimidate and harass people of color. That night, civil guard members said their mission was to protect Oñate.

Medina, enjoying a rare night home, was grilling hamburgers, his wife happy to finally have him around. Medina texted back and forth with his lieutenants at the museum. They told him about the civil guard being there and the pickaxe, but so far everything was peaceful.

Others at the protest didn't think so. New Mexico Civil Guard members were jockeying about like tough guys, fearlessly rattling long rifles and pistols like sabers. Reports of a guard member aiming his gun at protesters spread. Several people called 911, afraid of what these intimidators, armed to the teeth, might do. Michelle Melendez was there. The armed militia members were dangerous and scaring people, and police were nowhere in sight. The guard were the "armed friendlies" talked about on police scanners earlier that month.

APD's Lieutenant Pierson watched the militia members ruefully. They had already been told thanks, but no thanks, let the professionals handle the situation. Despite rebuttal, here they were again.

"This will turn out really bad if those jokers assault the protesters," APD spokesman Gilbert Gallegos texted. "Even the intimidation is troubling. Any ideas about de-escalating and getting them to back down?"

Chief Medina responded, "We are planning it, stay neutral."

In a matter of minutes, that all changed, but it wasn't a member of the guard who caused chaos to erupt and bullets to fly. Guard members had already begun to back away, while some of the protesters, many swarming the rocky hill on which Oñate stood, tried in vain to bring down the statue. Just after 8 p.m., video taken by protesters at the scene showed a man in a blue shirt shove or yank down at least two women, hurling them hard to the ground. Other protesters went after the man, who made a quick retreat, running, and stumbling. Someone smacked him with a purse. Someone threw a skateboard at him. The man in blue pulled out a gun and began firing. A protester later identified as thirty-nine year old Scott Williams went down with gunshot wounds to his torso.

It had all gone too far too fast. Lieutenant Pierson gave the command for the Emergency Response Team and quick-response team to move in. He estimates they were on scene in ninety seconds, an EMT from the quick-response team immediately rendering aid to the shooting victim. Within seven to nine minutes, the victim was in an ambulance on his way to the hospital.

The shooter—whom police identified as Steven Ray Baca, a failed city council candidate and the son of a Bernalillo County sheriff's deputy—was on his way to jail.

Medina was on his way to the dog house with his wife, leaving her and the hamburgers again to get to the scene, which had devolved into tear gas and chaos as officers attempted to disarm the guard and disperse the crowds, losing valuable evidence in the shooting as a result.

Mayor Keller was out jogging in the bosque when his phone started blowing up. "There's been a shooting," a text read. Keller ran home as fast as he could, changed clothes, and headed to city hall.

"I was worried about everything," he said.

Keller and CAO Sarita Nair were briefed on as much as was known about the shooting. At about 9:30 p.m., Keller issued his first order of the night: take down the Oñate statue.

"Someone could die if we don't take it down," Keller said. "I want it down by 8 a.m. tomorrow."

The mayor issued a statement to the public: "The shooting tonight was a tragic, outrageous, and unacceptable act of violence, and it has no place in our city. Our diverse community will not be deterred by acts meant to divide or silence us. Our hearts go out to the victim, his family, and witnesses whose lives were needlessly threatened tonight. This sculpture has now become an urgent matter of public safety. In order to contain the public safety risk, the city will be removing the statue until the appropriate civic institutions can determine next steps."

Keller called shooting victim Scott Williams' parents. Williams was in critical but stable condition in the hospital. He would likely survive, but it would be a long and painful recovery. The next day, the Williams family issued a statement of its own.

"When Steven Baca repeatedly attacked peaceful protesters in Albuquerque last night, Scott took bullets for the community he cares about," Williams' family wrote. "While he did, the Albuquerque Police Department hid behind the Albuquerque Museum, refused to respond to multiple requests for help, and only sent officers in once shots were fired."

The family's sentiment was echoed by many in the community who questioned once again the way APD had handled the situation. It felt again to Chief Medina like a case of damned if you do, damned if you don't.

"In this line of work, we always play for a tie," Medina said. "There was no win."

In fact, it felt like losing.

*The source's name has been changed to protect his identity.

12

Toward Healing

It's wrong to think that violence, tear gas, and trauma were all that emerged from the protests that filled city streets, including in Albuquerque, during the summer of 2020. Although the clashes and chaos made the headlines, most of the other fifty or so protests and gatherings that took place in Albuquerque were peaceful and productive.

"Multiple groups came together to bring attention to the issues that movements such as Black Lives Matter were bringing forward, and to focus only on the violent incidents minimizes that," said Michelle Melendez, director of the City of Albuquerque's Office of Equality and Inclusion. "Hundreds upon hundreds of people came together, and what they showed was unity and a dialog that we need to continue having." To Melendez, the summer of rage was also a summer of voices, speaking loudly and clearly about life at the crossroads. Melendez was determined to get city hall to listen.

"From dozens of meetings between Black Lives Matter organizers and the mayor and his staff these past weeks, we have listened, and, as the mayor has heard you say, we need a better way," Melendez wrote in a message to the public in the summer of 2020.

One of those ways was to introduce the Keller administration's proposal to send trained professionals to respond to certain police callouts, rather than armed officers. Mayor Keller announced that the Albuquerque Community Safety Department (ACS), believed to be the first of its kind in the country, would employ social workers, housing and homelessness specialists, and violence prevention and diversion program experts to service calls for certain mental health crises, housing needs, and general down-and-out situations.

Albuquerque Community Safety Department

THE RIGHT RESPONSE AT THE RIGHT RIGHT TIME.

→ The first-of-its-kind cabinet-level department will respond to calls and do outreach for inebriation, homelessness, addiction, and mental health.

→ Refocusing millions of dollars through budget process

→ Third option for 911 dispatch alongside APD and AFR

→ Unique Albuquerque idea based on programs we developed and tested with community

WHAT IT IS	WHAT IT IS NOT
Investing in behavioral health and community	Not taking money away from core police work or existing reform efforts
Shifting to a public health approach to poverty and trauma	Not turning away from our city's crime challenges
Focusing police officers' time on violent crime	Not deprioritizing crime fighting
Investing in community policing, diversion programs and violence intervention	Not ignoring the shortage of officers in our department
Emphasizing the core job description of police officers as 'guardians'	Not burdening officers with more tasks not related to core job
Investing resources in a non-police response	Not ignoring the massive budget cuts that APD suffered in the last recession
Responding to calls in a more cost-effective and sustainable way than police working alone	Not asking police to do more and more without giving them more resources
Building more than just another hotline or token gesture	Not pretending that people will stop calling 911 or needing a first responder

The Albuquerque Community Safety Department was created June 15, 2020. Informational graphic courtesy Albuquerque Community Safety Department.

Clockwise, from left: Harold Medina, APD, Mayor Tim Keller, Sylvester Stanley, ACS interim Superintendent of Police Reform and Deputy Chief Administrative Officer, and Sarita Nair, Chief Administrative Officer. Photo courtesy Mayor's Office, City of Albuquerque.

"It is fascinating that given all the challenges in America over the last one hundred years on a number of fronts, when it comes to public safety we still just think there's two departments—police and fire—in every city," Keller told the Associated Press in June 2020. "I think fundamentally this could be a new model for how we look at public safety response in cities across the country."

Melendez called the Albuquerque Community Safety Department a "safety net system" especially for the city's most vulnerable and stereotyped.

"The establishment of this new department acknowledges the mismatch between the social needs of people experiencing nonviolent crises and the existing infrastructure that attempts to respond to those needs. A social work response, rooted in social justice, gives us a much better chance of connecting people with the help they need and getting better outcomes for people of color without involving law enforcement," she wrote.

"This is key," Melendez continued. "People of color don't need more interactions with law enforcement. They know what they need—and they have told us many times. It is time we listen, and we are listening. Just like the city cannot wait for the county or anyone else to step up to the plate, we in the community, too, cannot wait any longer to build our collective capacity to meet the people's needs."

Then APD chief, Mike Geier, also approved of the idea, telling the *Washington Post* that police officers were "relieved" at the idea that some of their calls would shift to the new department.

Not surprisingly, not everybody was relieved or happy. Some called the idea a cheap shot against an already beleaguered, underfunded, and understaffed police department. Opponents lumped in the new ACS department with the polarizing "defund the police" slogan that had become a battlecry at protests across the country.

"It infuriates me," Albuquerque Police Officers' Association president Shaun Willoughby said in an interview with Albuquerque's KOAT-TV, a reversal of his initial view if cautious optimism about the idea. "We've been understaffed here for the last ten years, we're fighting to get to a level just to respond to the needs of the community. Police are a conduit to everything, and they're a conduit to a lot of things that society hasn't really done very good management of in general."

Willoughby's sentiments were echoed in the police union's annual "State of Policing Survey" released in July 2020 that found that 80% of the officers who responded had considered a new line of work in the past couple of months. Of those, 84% said it was because of the "current view on policing, the increased scrutiny on officers, new reform efforts, and job insecurity."

As 2020's summer of rage turned into the autumn of discontent, one of the most insecure jobs was APD chief, Mike Geier's. On September 10, 2020, the mayor announced that Geier was retiring after "righting the ship" during the first year of the Keller administration. Chief Geier thanked Keller for the honor to lead APD for three years but that after forty-seven years in law enforcement, said it was "time to pass the baton." Only later did Geier claim that the baton had been yanked out of his hand by Mayor Keller and CAO Sarita Nair, whom Geier blamed for micromanaging his duties.

"I'm not a cop anymore," Geier told the *Albuquerque Journal*. "I'm just a politician's aide is the way I describe it."

The City will be making its case in an upcoming lawsuit that these are the claims of a disgruntled former employee and has declined to speak specifically about Geier, voicing only sadness at his accusations and suggesting that the job of chief requires someone present and available, especially for the bigger incidents such as the violent outbursts that had broken out that summer.

"We rarely saw the chief," Mayor Keller said. "We can all agree that he wasn't there."

One member of APD who was there at every major incident was Harold Medina. After a national search to replace Geier, Medina was handed the chief's baton—and the chief's headaches. The promotion added to what Medina was already referring to as the most challenging year in his long career.

"We started out literally guarding toilet paper during the first days of this pandemic to dealing with the most protests this city has ever seen," Medina said of 2020. "What we do now is not normal."

Detail from a Paint for Peace mural at the KiMo Theater summer of 2020. Photo courtesy Mayor's office, City of Albuquerque.

From her vantage point, Victoria Van Dame can see much of the comings and goings along Central Avenue on the western edge of downtown Albuquerque from her nonprofit, OT Circus, a gallery space that combines art with therapy and community. The gallery's storefront looks onto the northwest side of Central near Seventh Street, with Van Dame's home directly in the back. The Curious Toast Cafe, which Van Dame also owns, sits on the southwest side of Central near Eighth Street.

Van Dame and her husband sat on the rooftop of OT Circus on the night of June 1, 2020, and watched protesters fill the streets during one of the first Black Lives Matter events since the death of George Floyd six days before.

"It was very peaceful, very uplifting," she said. That peaceful, uplifting feeling changed after the streets thinned of protesters and a new, rowdier, violent crowd descended upon downtown. "These weren't Black Lives Matter people," Van Dame said of the interlopers. "These were just angry people doing stupid things."

As the night wore on, Van Dame's husband sat inside OT Circus, shooing away people who were pressing hard against the large glass window in apparent attempts to break it. The couple could hear glass shattering in the distance, smell the fires and, later, tear gas. They could see riot gear-clad Albuquerque police gathering in preparation to break up what had become a violent free-for-all downtown and the near destruction of the KiMo Theatre two blocks east of their gallery. The next day, downtown was in shambles. City workers were everywhere, cleaning up debris, putting up large wooden boards over windows, both broken and intact, including the windows of OT Circus.

"It was like Armageddon," Van Dame said.

On a walk that afternoon, she spotted two young men spray painting one of the boards on a building on Fourth Street.

"They had this look on their faces, like, 'Oh shit, we're caught,'" Van Dame said, "but I went up to them and said that I'd rather look at their work than at an empty board, and that I had boards at my gallery. Would they like to come paint my boards?"

They did. That was the beginning of what became Paint for Peace 505, an impromptu art fest and a spontaneous gathering of street artists who were given a plethora of wooden canvases on which to express themselves and share their art in downtown Albuquerque in the summer of 2020. Word quickly spread through the street art community and on social media, and soon dozens of artists were showing up to claim a board and start creating, using their own paint or supplies OT Circus donated to them.

"This project really blew up into something bigger than we could have imagined," Van Dame said. "It wasn't anything we advertised or organized or controlled. It was the community coming together."

In two weeks in the summer of 2020, some forty-five artists took 175 boards from First to Eighth Streets in downtown Albuquerque and transformed them from ugly reminders of destruction and desolation to an outdoor art gallery filled with talent, joy, and unity. Paint for Peace 505 featured a wide range of styles, subjects, media, and meaning: a portrait of Malcolm X in shades of gray, cartoon Martians, anime heroines, ponies, butterflies, skulls, hearts, white and brown hands clasping each other. The art conveyed messages: cultivate tolerance. Stay cute and wash your hands. Abolish modern slavery. Make love your weapon. And justice for all. Hope. One painting featured a man with a backpack surveying the vista and the words: I am going to make it through this year if it kills me. The painting covering the large window of OT Circus portrayed the image of Chilean activist-musician Victor Jara and the lyrics to his anthem, "El derecho de vivir en paz." The right to live in peace.

Among the most prolific artists to share his work downtown was Nazario Sandoval, known for his lively streamers of color that he calls "squiggles."

"It's a healing process, and it's just sad that everyone broke these windows when this is a staple of the city," Sandoval said as he applied the squiggles to boards in front of the KiMo Theatre. "There's just so much rage and anger right now. I just think we need to heal and I think by art, and it doesn't matter who you are or what color you are, we can all relate to it and that's really where it is."

Detail from one of Nazario Sandoval's Paint for Peace murals on an Albuquerque business shut down during the summer of 2020. Photo courtesy of the Mayor's Office, City of Albuquerque.

Van Dame called the experience of Paint for Peace 505 magical.

"It was such positivity and unity," she said. "Downtown needs love, and this was love, and it didn't cost an extravagant amount. Sometimes it's not the money you put in it; it's the heart you put in it."

On July 17, 2020, the public was invited to tour the artwork, a welcome return to a part of the city that had been brutalized and bashed that summer. But like everything in 2020, Paint for Peace 505 was not without its criticism and chaos. Some in the community, particularly those involved in the Black Lives Matter movement, saw the boarded up windows as blaming the movement for violence and as an indication that the city feared more violence was coming. Some businesses felt the boards made the area look blighted. Some did not care for the artwork that graced their buildings. Tenants had not been consulted or asked whether they wanted their boards painted, said Dr. Shelle Sanchez, director of the City of Albuquerque Department of Arts & Culture.

"What was a spontaneous act of art and beauty was more complicated than that," Sanchez said. "Nothing was simple in 2020."

Flare-ups between artists cropped up. Among those who drew the ire of other artists was Nazario Sandoval, who some argued was hogging too many of the boards. Sandoval, who had been so supportive of Paint for Peace 505, distanced himself from the project and from Van Dame as a result.

"The aftermath became a bad thing in some ways," Van Dame said. "Still, it was such a good project." As the summer of 2020 faded, the art from Paint for Peace 505 and the boards came down, many of the works stored in a building downtown in the hopes of one day finding a place again to share the art.

"It would be a shame to have this all torn down and be lost," Van Dame said.

In Old Town, another work of art remained torn down, possibly for good. Mayor Keller had ordered the massive bronze statue of the controversial Don Juan de Oñate to be removed from its place at the front of the *La Jornada* installation near the Albuquerque Museum on the morning after the protest there June 15, 2020, had turned violent and resulted in the shooting of one participant. Taking down the statue was a quick response to prevent further bloodshed, but even before the shooting, the pain, pride, and controversy surrounding Oñate and *La Jornada* had again become an issue the city couldn't ignore.

"There was a need for a conversation in the city about how we represent our history," said Michelle Otero, former Albuquerque poet laureate, writer, and community facilitator. "Such conversations were being held across the country after the death of George Floyd, especially in the south where monuments to Confederate icons are common. Here, we don't have monument rows like Richmond, Virginia, but we have Oñate and *La Jornada*. Oñate, in many ways, was New Mexico's Robert E. Lee."

Otero, a New Mexico native who conducts racial equality and healing work around the country, knew what Dr. Sanchez was calling about even before she uttered the first word about helping the city determine what to do about Oñate. "It was time," Otero said. Not only did Dr. Sanchez ask Otero to be lead facilitator for what became the Race, History and Healing Project, but Otero was tasked with designing how it would work. What Otero hadn't expected was that the time she would have to complete the project would be so short—about three months.

"It seemed too little time and too polarizing a subject to do this," Otero fretted. "But at the same time, I thought, what an opportunity to have this conversation."

Any conversation, however, was still stymied by COVID-19, which had not miraculously gone away. On July 30, 2020, Governor Lujan Grisham extended New Mexico's emergency public health orders prohibiting mass gatherings and requiring masks in public. That same day, New Mexico officials reported 255 new cases of COVID-19 across the state, sixty-three of them in Bernalillo County for a total of 4,688 cases in the county since March 2020.

Race, History, and Healing Project team, courtesy Mayor's Office City of Albuquerque. Dr. Shelle Sanchez, Marisa Leger, Terry Sloan, Alicia Manzano, Diana Delgado, Huitzil Bennett-Perez, Hakim Bellamy. Back: Michelle Melendez, Dr. Josie Lopez, Veronica Archuleta, Tanya Lenti, Alan Armijo, Diego Lucero. Photo courtesy of the Arts and Culture Department, City of Albuquerque.

The Race, History and Healing Project introduced several ways for the community—young, old, all ethnicities and cultures, all genders, all religions—to participate through online community group conversation sessions led by facilitators, surveys, and short interviews. For the group conversations, participants were asked to commit to attending three sessions, each two hours, for the full two-hour session. It was a slow process done faster than Otero might have liked, each participant in the group conversation gently allowed first to feel that they would be heard and that they would listen to others.

"We created a 'container' where all felt safe, and we practiced listening to each other, even those we disagreed with, and sharing space," Otero said of the process. "We wanted participants to just sit with each other as human beings."

The discussions did not begin with the hot button issue of Oñate and what to do about the statue. Rather, participants were asked to contemplate three topics. First, they were asked to share a story in which they felt their race or culture was affirmed. Then, they were asked to recall one of their first teachers, whether in school or of family or community, and a value that teacher shared with them. Finally, they were asked how they saw themselves and their community and culture represented in public spaces.

"The idea was for them to see the common values each of them may share before moving on to what was likely the more divisive territory," Otero said.

District 1 City Councilor Lan Sena, members of the CROWN Coalition Committee, Mayor Tim Keller, and Managing Assistant City Attorney Torri A. Jacobus at the signing of the CROWN Act. Photo courtesy Mayor's Office, City of Albuquerque.

There were those participants who, when the issue of the statue was finally broached, strongly believed that Oñate was a part of their culture and should not be taken away. There were others who felt so much pain just knowing *La Jornada* existed that they refused to go anywhere near Mountain and 19th where the installation was situated.

"There were numerous moments facilitators had to interrupt to redirect the conversation," Otero said. "I remember one person who was very pro-Oñate who told the group, 'If you take this away it's just one more thing taken away from us,' and I thought, there's the wound, there's the need."

A woman from Acoma Pueblo also felt the wound caused by loss when as a child she was forbidden to speak her native language in school.

Participants began to see they shared common feelings, and if they could feel that, maybe they could begin to understand each other's point of view.

"They came from different places and different views, yet through this process they learned they shared some of the same feelings and values," Otero said. "We heard from some participants afterward who told us the process was worthwhile, even those who did not like the outcome."

In the end, the Race, History and Healing Project held fifty-nine community conversations with 241 participants. Hundreds more participated in 1,290 surveys and 117 interviews. The report found that a majority agreed that the Oñate statue should not be returned to public view and that *La Jornada* should be "re-envisioned and re-contextualized." Exactly how remains unclear. In October 2020, the Albuquerque Arts Board voted in support of the project's recommendation and presented it to the City Council.

"We launched the project this summer knowing that tensions were high and the community needed a place to have these hard conversations," Keller said in an October 30, 2020, news release announcing the Race, History and

Because of 2020, July 3, 2020. Photo by Jessica Roybal, courtesy Albuquerque Museum Digital Archives, object # PA2021.032.004

Artist Jodie Herrera in front of one of her City of Albuquerque Public Art murals created during the pandemic, with Mayor Keller and artists represented. Photo courtesy Mayor's Office, City of Albuquerque.

Healing Project report. "Any process like this that aims to bring people with different perspectives together will be difficult and complex, but it was also a powerful way to engage over 1,500 people, many of whom were part of the 130 hours of dialogue, because they care so deeply about our community and how we represent our diverse cultures and histories."

On December 7, 2020, the Albuquerque City Council punted, choosing not to accept or reject the recommendations from the report and suggesting that further public input was needed once the pandemic abated.

"This is one of those things we shouldn't rush into," Albuquerque City Councilor Trudy Jones told the *Albuquerque Journal*.

As 2020 came to a close, the debate on the Oñate statue was once again put on hold, more than twenty-two years after it began.

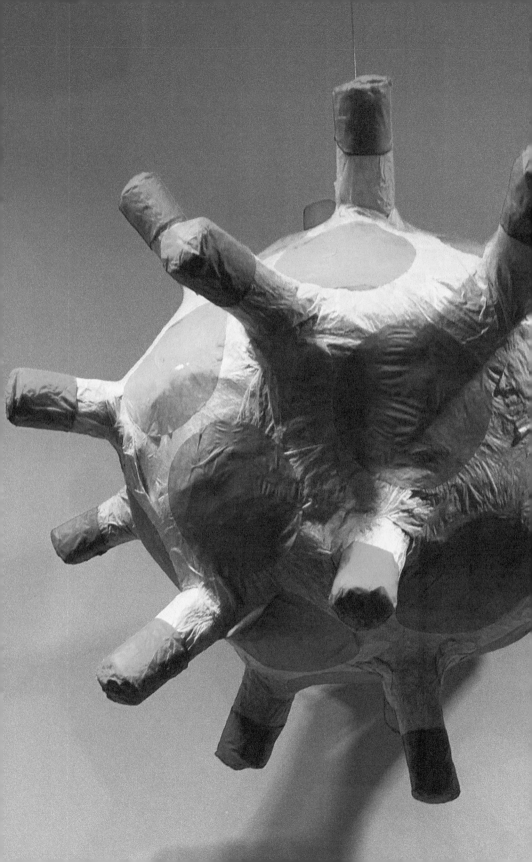

13

The Good, the Bad, and the Autumn

For many people, 2020 meant staying home, their offices and their children's schools relocated to their kitchen tables, living rooms truly the room where nearly all living occurred. It was the new normal shared by Mayor Keller and his wife, Dr. Elizabeth Kistin Keller, a Rhodes Scholar and systems research analyst at Sandia National Laboratories. Both Mayor and First Lady Keller juggled increased pandemic-related workloads that kept them busier than ever. As parents to two young children, the Kellers' situation at times felt disquieting, challenging, and required some fancy scheduling and child-care wizardry.

Despite long workdays, during the pandemic the Kellers tried to make it home in time to have dinner with their kids, Jack and Maya, and spend some evening time as a family every day. But after the children were tucked in bed, it was back to work for both Kellers, answering calls and emails, doing interviews, reading, researching, putting out fires.

During the weekdays, First Lady Keller juggled the children's virtual homeschooling with work. The mayor crafted his schedule around parenting duties, conducting meetings in parking lots, over Zoom and phone, with the children in tow. In between his daily mayoral duties, Mayor Keller traveled with the children to nearby locations where he could just be Dad for a couple of hours.

"I looked for places where we could be alone out of the pressure cooker," Keller said. "The mountains, Tijeras, Madrid, playgrounds—anywhere we could get to in two hours."

At each destination du jour, Mayor Keller picked up takeout for the family dinner. Cheese and Coffee in Albuquerque, El Bruno's in Cuba, or

Rumor Brewing Co. in Cedar Crest. Mayor Keller's epicurean adventures became "Tim's Takeout," a running bit at the end of his daily news briefings with him giving a plug to the restaurant cooking for him and the family that night.

"It was just something nice in a time that was not always so nice," Keller said.

September 2020, though, was turning out to be a pretty nice month, relatively speaking. Optimism was in the air, and finally it seemed like New Mexico and its largest city were turning the corner on the coronavirus pandemic. New Mexico was one of only a handful of states doing well in September 2020, meeting all four of the necessary gating criteria for loosening state public health orders—reducing spread rate, testing, contact tracing, and healthcare system capacity.

As summer of 2020 ended, New Mexico restaurants and breweries were allowed to operate at 25% capacity indoors, travel quarantine was eased, hotels were allowed to operate at 75% maximum capacity, and some schools were allowed to reopen under a hybrid part in-person, part virtual model. On September 9, 2020, New Mexico hit its lowest rolling average of COVID-19 cases since April 2020. That day, the New Mexico Department of Health reported ninety-two new cases, six in Bernalillo County.

"We were feeling that all the systems we put in place and all the decisions that were made on a state, but also a local level, were paying off, and Albuquerque was in good shape, financially and otherwise," Keller said. "Credit goes to the team and city employees and, most importantly, the citizens of Albuquerque."

That same day, the Albuquerque City Council unanimously approved two measures important to the Keller administration. Resolutions 20-75 and 20-83, co-sponsored by Councilors Klarissa Peña, Cynthia Borrego, and Lan Sena. The resolutions strengthened the city's commitment to addressing racial equity and social justice and establishing a foundation for improving equity in city policy, processes, programs, and service delivery.

"With these resolutions, we assure that the work we started continues whether or not Mayor Keller wins a second term in 2021," said Michelle Melendez, who played a major role in the development of the resolutions. "We are working to improve our community's outcomes so that race is no longer a predictor of one's health, wealth, and safety."

Mayor Keller and his team were on a roll, and it appeared Albuquerque residents were happy enough to keep rolling with them. An *Albuquerque Journal* poll released in September 2020 found that 60% of Albuquerque residents approved of Keller's performance nearly three years into his first term as mayor. That was just shy of the 61% approval rating he received in 2018 after his first nine months in office. In spite of the pandemic and the violence in the city, Keller was still earning honeymoon-level numbers.

An additional *Journal* poll also found that 60% of New Mexico voters approved of Governor Lujan Grisham's handling of the COVID-19 response,

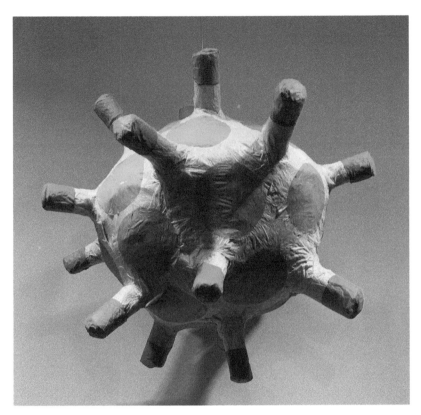

Coronavirus symbols and graphics were everywhere during the pandemic; even in time honored traditions like the piñata. Photo courtesy Albuquerque Museum

while 55% disapproved of President Trump's handling of the pandemic.

Later in September 2020, the annual city-funded "citizen satisfaction survey" was released, and once again Mayor Keller and other city officials received high marks for their performance during the pandemic, 61% believing that Albuquerque was in better hands than other cities in the country.

"This year's survey revealed significant support for the city's pandemic response, with Mayor Keller taking the lead and effectively communicating with the public throughout the crisis," said Brian Sanderoff, president of Research and Polling, Inc., the firm that conducted the survey.

The survey also gave high marks to the Keller administration for its efforts to address civil rights, equity, and inclusion issues. Police, too, earned high numbers in spite of low morale among officers and the messy handling of Chief Geier's dismissal. What Keller said he was most proud of, though, was that despite the pandemic and the protests and the teetering economy, he and his team had kept the city running. Albuquerque had adequate coffers and no need to furlough any of the roughly 6,000 city employees—luxuries many other U.S. city governments could not enjoy.

Travelers in the ABQ Sunport mock the state's public health order and mask mandates. Photo courtesy of the Mayor's Office, City of Albuquerque.

"Within two weeks of the pandemic, we took strong measures to cut costs and hunker down for the long run," Keller told citizens in a September 3, 2020, news release. "While times are going to still be tough for the city, we are one of the most prepared in the nation to weather this corona storm."

Keller pointed to a *New York Times* article as proof of Albuquerque's rosier economic position relative to other large cities. The article, published August 16, 2020, referred to a study in the *National Tax Journal* in which Albuquerque ranked the second-lowest out of forty cities in terms of revenue shortfalls expected because of the pandemic recession. Albuquerque fared better, according to the analysis, because its economy relies more heavily on stable revenue and property taxes, rather than tourist dollars or sales taxes.

City of Albuquerque Chief Financial Officer, Sanjay Bhakta, also credited the city's robust pre-pandemic economy, $150 million in federal relief funding, and a new internet sales tax stream with keeping shortfalls slim. Despite the city's successes, though, gross receipts tax revenue for fiscal year 2020, which ended June 30, finished nearly 5% behind projections. While that was better than expected, it still meant $19.9 million less than anticipated before COVID-19 came to town.

"It meant maybe we have fewer zoning inspections or longer times between maintaining city parks," Keller said. "It meant a hiring freeze and no cost of living raises."

Any celebration or sighs of relief in city hall and elsewhere, however, were short lived. Even as residents started easing back into a more normal existence, the coronavirus was beginning to churn up again, the result of Labor Day gatherings in which mask-wearing and social distancing were not adhered to and the loosening of restrictions.

Firefighters commemorate 9/11 in 2020 with COVID-safe precautions. Photo courtesy Mayor's Office, City of Albuquerque.

"People just started becoming too comfortable, too ready to drop their guards," Mayor Keller said, "and the results were bad." By September 22, 2020, COVID-19 was starting to spread slightly more rapidly than the state's target, according to the Department of Health. New Mexico reported 110 new cases, twenty-one of those in Bernalillo County.

"We knew it was going to go up," New Mexico Human Services Secretary David Scrase said. "The question is, what's it going to do in the next week or two? If it continues to go up, we're going to have to think about how to respond to that."

By September 30, 2020, New Mexico reported 281 new COVID-19 cases, the most in a single day since infections peaked in late July 2020 and more than twice the average since right after Labor Day. Of those, sixty-one cases were from Bernalillo County.

"Please take this virus seriously," Governor Lujan Grisham tweeted. "COVID-19 is not through with us."

On October 9, 2020, New Mexico reported 488 new cases of COVID-19—a record for daily cases since the first days of the pandemic seven months earlier. Bernalillo County reported 135 new cases. Those numbers did not dissuade about 250 student athletes, coaches, and parents who that same day staged a protest in northeast Albuquerque against the governor's decision to cancel New Mexico's fall high school sports activities because of the rising cases of coronavirus.

"It's time we relied on the families to make decisions for their kids, and not an elected official who's only going to be here for one term," La Cueva

Balloon Fall Fest launch in 2020. 2020 was the only year the Balloon Fiesta was not held in its fifty-year history. Photo courtesy of the Mayor's Office, City of Albuquerque.

High School football coach Brandon Back told the *Albuquerque Journal*. "We're falling apart at the seams, it feels like."

Five days later, New Mexico reported 577 new COVID-19 case numbers, 199 of them in Bernalillo County. Two days after that, the numbers soared to 819 new cases, 178 of them in Bernalillo County. It was only getting worse.

"We are so doomed," local epidemiologist Maria Montgomery* wrote on October 16, 2020, on Facebook. Montgomery, who had become something of a social media heroine for her straight talk and simple way of helping others navigate COVID-19, explained that the new numbers indicated that New Mexico had reached exponential growth of the virus.

"There is no controlling it at this point," she said. "The hard truth is that with over 800 cases, we just don't have enough resources. We are trying our hardest, but there are only so many people at DOH, even with all the added contact tracers and case investigators. We can't perform effective contact tracing on over 1,000 cases a day—and I'd bet money that we cross 1,000 cases a day next week." She wasn't too far off. Thirteen days after her "bet," New Mexico reported 1,082 new cases in a single day.

Montgomery speculated that the COVID-19 calamity was caused in part on the decision weeks before to ease travel restrictions, which allowed residents to bring back more than souvenirs from high-risk areas of the country. "That, combined with COVID fatigue where people are spending tons of time unmasked in small gatherings with their friends, just has put us in a very tough position," she said.

*The source's name has been changed to protect her identity.

Balloon Fall Fest launch in October 2020. Photo courtesy of the Mayor's Office, City of Albuquerque.

Governor Lujan Grisham apparently agreed with that speculation, tightening public health orders that same day that included mandatory quarantine for out of state visitors to New Mexico—quarantine that could be as long as two weeks if one was coming from a high-risk place. In addition, the governor ordered all food and drink establishments and liquor stores to close by 10 p.m. nightly, prohibited mass gatherings of more than five, and reduced hotel occupancy from between 60% to 25%, depending on whether the establishment had completed a COVID-19 safety training program.

"This is the most severe emergency New Mexico has ever faced," Lujan Grisham said. "I cannot be more clear: The moment to turn the tide has to be right now, immediately, or else we face accelerating significant illnesses and needless deaths for hundreds of New Mexicans. The state will be forced to hunker back down. The health and economic consequences caused by the continued out-of-control spread of the virus will be devastating."

Less than a week later, Mayor Keller issued his own mandate, warning that the City of Albuquerque was ready to crack down on citizens failing to adhere to the state public health orders.

"We are going to be drastically ramping up enforcement under the existing public health order," Keller said during an October 21, 2020, news briefing. "There's nothing new here. We have just got to make sure we do a better job of actually following that public health order."

Nearly every day, the numbers of new COVID-19 cases and deaths broke records. On October 30, 2020, New Mexico hit one of its grimmest milestones, passing the 1,000 mark in COVID-19-related deaths since the beginning of the pandemic. Healthcare leaders voiced alarm at the rapid rise of cases in October and the numbers of COVID-19 cases filling up hospitals. Several warned that MASH-style units might need to be set up to handle the overflow of patients if the new cases continued at the same pace.

"The velocity of that spike is like nothing else we've seen in this pandemic," Dr. Jason Mitchell, Chief Medical Officer at the New Mexico-based Presbyterian Healthcare Services, said in an online news briefing. "This is a serious call to action for us as a community."

November 2020 was worse. In the first week, hospitals reported a record high of more than 400 hospitalizations as a result of COVID-19. Governor Lujan Grisham warned that New Mexico was running out of hospital beds and healthcare workers to handle the growing calamity. On November 7, the state's rolling average was in excess of 1,000 cases a day for the first time since the pandemic's earliest days. The state average of new cases was 1,027 a day, as compared to 276 cases just one month before. On November 12, 2020, new cases soared to 1,753, the average reaching nearly 1,400 cases a day. That day, eighteen more people were reported to have died because of COVID-19, the second deadliest day of the pandemic at the time.

"We are literally parking refrigerated trucks outside our Office of the Medical Investigator because we anticipate having so many deaths that they will run out of room," Montgomery told her social media followers. "I want you to think about what it would feel like to have your loved one's body in storage in a refrigerated truck. And then I want you to stay home."

Front-line workers were being especially hit hard, including the Albuquerque Police Department and Albuquerque Fire and Rescue, each department reporting spikes of COVID infections of at least twenty members apiece, with many more sidelined awaiting COVID-19 test results.

"We are doing our best to keep our officers safe, shutting down substations to the public, and asking the public to make non-emergency reports online," APD's Chief Medina said. "This virus is pretty tough, and it's hitting us across the board."

Among those infected by COVID-19 in November 2020 was Brandon Back, the La Cueva High School football coach who a month before had protested the governor's cancellation of fall high school sports in New Mexico.

"The whole family had it," Back told an *Albuquerque Journal* sports columnist of his COVID-19 infection. "I had one bad day where I felt really crappy. And I was achy for a few days after that." He and his wife, Back said, also lost their sense of taste and smell, his wife's symptoms lasting for six weeks.

On November 16, 2020, the governor got tougher on the virus, mandating a two-week lockdown on in-person dining, salons, gyms, and other "nonessential" businesses across the state. She called it a "reset," an

Mayor Keller at APD's Real Time Crime Center on Election Day, 2020. Photo courtesy of the Mayor's Office, City of Albuquerque.

apparent attempt to sprinkle sugar on a very bitter pill.

"We are at the breaking point, quite frankly," Governor Lujan Grisham said in announcing her orders during an online news conference.

The next day, New Mexico reported twenty-eight deaths associated with COVID-19—another record. A day after that, the state reached a terrifying 3,675 new cases—also another record. That day, new cases in Bernalillo County exploded to 993, from 615 cases the previous day.

Three days before Thanksgiving, City of Albuquerque officials announced that with COVID-19 still blowing up across the city, there was no other choice than to cancel its popular holiday events, including the River of Lights display at the ABQ BioPark, the Twinkle Light Parade through Nob Hill, the ABQ Ride Luminaria Tour through the Country Club neighborhood and Old Town, the public Old Town tree lighting ceremony, Shop and Stroll in Nob Hill, and the New Year's Eve Before Dark festivities.

The city's holiday cancellations added to the growing list of popular events Albuquerque residents had lost in 2020, among them the Gathering of Nations Powwow, the Freedom 4th fireworks, the New Mexico State Fair, the Albuquerque International Balloon Fiesta, Duke City Marathon, New Mexico United soccer games, Albuquerque Isotopes baseball games, college

Mayor Keller with COO Lawrence Rael and Deputy of Economic Development, Synthia Jaramillo, introducing the new cleaning robot at the SunPort.

and high school sports, and local theater. COVID-19 was also gnawing away at the holiday season. Thanksgiving feasts around the city were likely to be much smaller gatherings, or no gathering at all, given the governor's reset.

Montgomery had little sympathy.

"I'm still at work right now, trying to help someone who is (COVID-19) positive find a place to stay to keep her elderly family members safe," she told social media followers on November 25, 2020, the day before Thanksgiving. "A coworker is a few feet away trying to figure out how to get body bags to a hospital because they have literally run out. We are both working tomorrow, too. So let's just be totally clear: If you are planning on posting photos of fifteen people sitting around a Thanksgiving table, inside, with no masks on, you might want to make a special filter so that none of the epidemiologists and medical professionals you know see them. We are exhausted and missing Thanksgiving with our own families to try to keep you safe. The least you could do to repay that sacrifice is stay home."

Ever the optimist, Mayor Keller addressed the residents of Albuquerque in a Thanksgiving address, acknowledging the devastation and frustration of a very bad year but taking stock in what he—and, he hoped, they—were thankful for.

With an increased focus on sanitizing public spaces, the City of Albuquerque employed a cleaning robot at the Albuquerque International Sunport. Photo courtesy City of Albuquerque.

"2020 has looked very different than we all thought it would," Keller wrote in his letter, published November 26 in the *Albuquerque Journal*. "For so many, this year has brought the toughest challenges of our lives. Still, on this Thanksgiving, I am more thankful than ever to live in Albuquerque. Over the past year Burqueños demonstrated that we adapt quickly and unite to keep each other safer and healthier. Most of us are doing our part by wearing our masks, distancing and staying home. We remain true to our hometown values, seeking solace in our parks and open spaces, and dropping off groceries to our parents. As the safety net becomes a landing place for many of our residents, we step up to do more for those who are struggling in our community.

"As shutdowns swept the nation, many cities and counties closed City Hall, and along with it, important services their residents depend on. We knew we had to carve our own path. We swung open the doors of our community centers to provide free COVID-safe child care for healthcare and other front-line workers. We bolstered our Westside Emergency Housing Center, brought in a medical team and COVID testing, offered three hot meals a day, and for many months avoided the large-scale, unstoppable outbreaks that many cities saw. And we didn't wait for even more folks to become homeless; we ramped up rental assistance and worked to halt evictions to keep more people in their homes.

"We are grateful for our local partners and city departments who have made all the difference. Hotel partners stepped up to house the homeless, healthcare workers, and first responders who needed to isolate. Our Senior Affairs Department found safe ways to break through loneliness with virtual

Mayor Keller lights a candle at a vigil for victims of COVID-19 on Civic Plaza. Photo courtesy Mayor's Office, City of Albuquerque.

programming, meal delivery, and wellness checks, and by providing more than half a million meals with top-notch drive-up services at our senior centers. Our state leadership and DOH have kept testing going in the face of great challenges. Albuquerque healthcare providers have been caring not just for us, but for much of New Mexico.

"While the streets were empty, we created construction industry jobs by fast-tracking more than $175 million in infrastructure projects including a new library, new community centers, and improvements to roads across the city. We secured federal CARES Act dollars to fund grants and PPE for our local business owners who have been hit hardest by this virus, and prevented layoffs and furloughs for city workers.

"In true One Albuquerque Spirit, many volunteers dedicated hours to making thousands of hand-made face masks for essential workers and vulnerable populations. Signs popped up in yards and on street corners with reminders that we will get through this together. Parades of colorfully decorated cars drove around hospitals, with people shouting their gratitude to our healthcare workers and best wishes for those who were sick.

"Like many of you, Liz and I start the day with precious moments with the kids at home, alongside the frustrations of getting them logged on and engaged for distance learning. On the weekends, we recall the things we did last year at this time and look for ways to stay connected with friends and family. We optimistically say, 'Next year in person for–insert special occasion.'

If we each do our part to stop the spread and look out for each other, we can make that hope a reality. This Thanksgiving, I am more thankful than ever to live in Albuquerque, and I know we will get through this together," Keller promised.

Tough days for Albuquerque and the rest of the state and the nation lay ahead, however. On December 17, 2020, New Mexico reached forty-eight deaths due to COVID-19, the highest reported in a single day. Slowly, though, New Mexico was finally turning a corner as 2020 hurtled toward its welcomed end. Numbers of new cases were beginning to fall, the governor's "reset" finally taking a tenuous hold. Burqueños began to embrace the notion of a weird Christmas but surely the last weird Christmas in the time of coronavirus. Weary eyes were already looking toward a new year—2021—a new presidential administration, and a new glimmer of hope.

By the end of 2020, vaccines against the novel coronavirus were already on the horizon, a medical miracle of sorts, produced in less than a year. The U.S. Food and Drug Administration approved a two-dose vaccine manufactured by Pfizer for emergency use on December 11, 2020. Two more vaccines—a two-dose version from Moderna and a single-dose version from Johnson and Johnson—were not far behind in gaining emergency use approval, on December 18, 2020, and February 27, 2021, respectively. Vaccines were, many health experts agreed, the best hope the world had of beating back this devastating virus.

Finally, a light—still distant, still obscured by misinformation, distrust, and political acrimony— was beginning to glow at the end of a very long tunnel.

Photo by Eric Williams, courtesy City of Albuquerque Arts & Culture

*Saving joy brought a sense of life as
it used to be, as it should be, as it would be,
fingers crossed, again. Saving joy brought hope.*

14

Saving Joy

Nearly fifty years ago, a humble young man sat in a room with longtime Old Town Albuquerque merchants as they hashed over business plans and philanthropic interests. The young man, in his twenties, was a rancher by trade from the Manzano Mountains who knew plenty about raising cattle but almost nothing about running a retail business. Yet there he was, the newest Old Town merchant, sitting with the old guard after putting money down on a small shop where he hoped to sell his father's hand-woven Chimayó style rugs and blankets. So he listened, and he learned.

He dared to imagine the day his little store would turn enough profit that he could raise a family comfortably and give back to the community generously, just like the old guard. With God's help and hard work, he vowed to make that happen. That humble young man was Henry Aceves, whose little store in 1973 grew into the Old Town Basket and Rug Shop and the Plaza Don Luis shopping mall, one of the largest retail complexes in the historic heart of Albuquerque.

Henry Aceves' businesses became even more successful than he had imagined, and his generosity was even greater than most people knew. Grandstanding was not Aceves' style. Quiet benevolence was. Perhaps his most celebrated gift is Albuquerque's official Christmas tree, the annual lighting of which draws thousands to Old Town and marks the official start of the holiday season in Albuquerque. Yet few know that Aceves is the city's secret Santa behind the beloved tree, which has been ranked by national publications as the tallest and best Christmas tree in New Mexico.

The tree is actually many trees—100-200 of them sized and fitted into the sleeves of a fifty-five foot steel structure, one of only two produced in the country. The structure was commissioned by another benevolent citizen, Albuquerque beer and bank business magnate, George Maloof Sr., who wanted the tree for the downtown plaza in front of First National Bank, of which he was majority shareholder in the 1970s. The tree made its debut to great fanfare and delight on the first Friday in December 1975 and became one of the city's biggest holiday attractions every year. Maloof owned the tree and provided the financial backing to bring it to life each year, but the citizens of Albuquerque adopted the tree as their own.

The Maloofs hired members of the Old Town Optimist Club to construct the massive tree, string lights, and hang ornaments. The members used the money they earned to pay for a Christmas party for underprivileged children. Days before the tree lighting in 1980, however, the Maloof dynasty lost its patriarch to a heart attack. George Maloof, Sr. was just fifty-seven years old when he died suddenly. The family sold off their banking interests in 1993 and gave the tree's frame to the Old Town Optimist Club. Without a benefactor, though, it appeared the tree was destined to become part of Christmases past.

Henry Aceves wouldn't hear of it. He had just broken ground that year for the Plaza Don Luis, a 32,000 square-foot retail space named in honor of his father. The plaza included a central courtyard, and it seemed to Aceves that it would be the perfect new home for the Christmas tree. The famous tree made its holiday debut there a year later. Just like Maloof, Aceves wanted the citizens of Albuquerque to feel that the tree was theirs and a part of the city's holiday tradition. Aceves also continued to quietly pay the Old Town Optimist Club's fee so the children's party they hosted could continue.

As the years passed, the club's membership aged and dwindled. Eventually, the club could no longer handle the duties of preparing the tree for its holiday showing. They fielded an offer from a Memphis business to purchase the steel tree structure and contemplated selling it for scrap metal. Aceves was determined to keep the tradition going, so he purchased the steel structure from the Old Town Optimist Club and enlisted members of his and wife Karen's large families to take over the tree duties.

The City of Albuquerque also pitched in, providing equipment and employees to help construct and decorate the tree. The city also shut down street traffic and provided crowd control when the throngs descended upon Old Town for the lighting ceremony and the city-sponsored Old Town Holiday Stroll, both held the first Friday in December each year. Aceves always made sure enough money was left over for holiday giving, distributing donations to several charities and causes, including the San Felipe de Neri Church, a few steps away from the tree in Old Town. Aceves fulfilled the vows he had made decades before, and in the merriest of ways. You might say that Aceves was the man who saved Christmas, at least a part of it, in Albuquerque.

Saving holidays and traditions and the other well-loved events that make Albuquerque such a unique place to live became much harder in 2020 as COVID-19 continued its march across the world. With health orders shutting down businesses, urging people to stay home or social distance in public, the holidays, big events, and traditions were bound to look anything but traditional—if they happened at all.

With so many crucial city services to keep running through the pandemic, it might have seemed like a trifling effort to worry much about parades and parties and Christmas tree lightings, but saving joy brought smiles at a time when smiles were not plentiful, when sickness and sadness and the specter of death were pervasive. Saving joy brought a sense of life as it used to be, as it should be, as it would be, fingers crossed, again. Saving joy brought hope.

"It was very important to us at city hall to carry on not just all the services a city provides, but to do what was possible, what was safe in terms of events," said Dr. Shelle Sanchez, director of Arts & Culture, the municipal department responsible for many of those events. "We didn't want to add to that sense of loss. We wanted to find ways to make people feel better."

Saving joy meant finding new ways to present time-honored, familiar events. As was true for every other department of the city, it meant finding ways to keep staff employed. For Arts & Culture it also meant finding ways to keep afloat those in the private sector connected to city events—artists, musicians, food vendors, restaurateurs, small business owners, face painters, and bounce house operators among them. That task fell, in large part, to Community Events Manager, Bree Ortiz, of Arts & Culture. Ortiz, energetic and public relations-savvy with a smile that never faded no matter how exhausting the day, had worked for the department for nine and a half years, and in late 2019 she was promoted to the division manager position. The year 2020 was going to be her biggest year thus far, and she was ready.

"I remember thinking about the new year and saying, 'OK, we are going to kick ass,'" she said.

Instead, 2020 nearly kicked hers and her small team of eleven. "We were kept in the loop even before all the shutdowns, because we knew whatever was coming for us was going to affect how we put on upcoming events and dealt with crowds," Ortiz said. "But I don't think in the beginning that we thought COVID was going to totally erase our whole calendar."

Week after week, Ortiz and her team started making the calls to cancel and close upcoming events and venues for the rest of March 2020. Then April. The KiMo. The Fiestas de Albuquerque in Old Town, which would have celebrated the city's 314th birthday in 2020. The Renaissance Faire at the Balloon Museum. The Rail Yards Market.

"Painful," Ortiz sighed. "We were returning deposits, canceling two and three weeks of events at a time. At first, we thought we could get by just postponing the events, but as time went on we knew we had to cancel most of them, because we just didn't know when we would ever go back to normal. We were so busy, always here, canceling."

It was shocking, like nothing she had ever imagined. By May 2020, with no end in sight to the pandemic, Ortiz and her team began to regroup and rethink how best to use the down time to everybody's benefit—remodeling the KiMo, for example—and how best to salvage what they could of the city's event calendar.

"We wanted to give people some sense of enjoyment, and we also wanted to find ways to still support artists and musicians and others whose livelihoods were now in jeopardy because of all the shutdowns," Ortiz said. "We wanted there to be an entertainment community still around when this was all over. If they don't exist, we don't, either."

The city's Arts & Culture team began making use of social media, posting concerts of local musicians on Facebook, paying performers to broadcast from the safety of their homes, the living room concerts livestreamed to the living rooms of the public. For the city's annual Zoo Concert Series, performances were livestreamed from the zoo bandshell with no one but the animals and a few staff on site to listen.

When the state's public health orders allowed, Ortiz's team supported a timed ticketing system at the ABQ BioPark, including at the zoo, in which a limited number of tickets went on sale daily. Visitors selected their arrival time and purchased their tickets in advance, thus keeping down crowd size and reducing wait times to enter. The team also created the Albuquerque Drive-Thru Grab & Go online shopping markets, five in all, from which artists, artisans, chefs, bakers, and other food providers sold their wares and customers picked up their purchases curbside at specific locations around town. Local musicians—always paid—provided entertainment for patrons waiting in their cars.

"It was a lot of work," Ortiz said of the initiatives, "but it worked."

Big events were reimagined. Albuquerque's Freedom Fourth, an extravaganza of food, concerts, and fireworks that draws 30,000-50,000 people to Balloon Fiesta Park each July 4 couldn't go on as it always had. Instead, David Simon, director of the City of Albuquerque Parks and Recreation Department, and his crew helped devise a fireworks display residents could watch safely from their homes, the fireworks launched from four locations in each quadrant of the city, all synchronized to music aired on KKOB's AM and FM stations.

"It was very well-received. It was safe. People seemed to appreciate it and follow the rules around it," Mayor Keller told the *Albuquerque Journal* afterward. "I think people also really appreciated the fact we did something."

Something had to happen to save the Albuquerque International Balloon Fiesta, the city's biggest and most beloved annual event, attracting hundreds of thousands of visitors from around the world over the course of nine days in October. It was hard to imagine Albuquerque in the fall without the earthy fragrances of piñon and roasting chile; hard to imagine crisper days and golden cottonwoods. Harder still to imagine morning skies and windless evenings without hundreds of balloons in every hue and shape.

The Balloon Fiesta, which USA Today calls the most photographed event in the world, not only fills the skies and thrills the eyes, but it also packs Albuquerque hotels, motels, restaurants, and shops. In 2019, the fiesta generated $186.8 million of total economic impact for businesses in the Albuquerque area and an estimated $4.1 million in tax dollars to the city of Albuquerque, according to a survey commissioned by the Balloon Fiesta and conducted by Forward Analytics, a national market research firm. The joy the fiesta brings to the crowds who crane their necks to take in the magical, colorful views is priceless, however. COVID-19 was prepared to burst the fiesta's balloon in 2020.

So the city's Parks and Recreation Department got busy. Following a similar idea that had worked successfully for the Freedom Fourth, they devised the Albuquerque Balloon Fall Fest, inviting local balloonists to launch at public golf courses and parks across the metro area on certain mornings in October.

"We believe Albuquerque families still deserve, and should, see balloons in the sky in the fall," Keller said.

And they did. Balloons went up, but COVID-19 numbers were still up, too, and that meant the number of events needing to be canceled wasn't going down—and the holidays were coming. Canceled already were the River of Lights display at the ABQ BioPark, the Twinkle Light Parade in Nob Hill, and the ABQ Ride Luminaria Tour, the latter so popular that the 3,000 tickets available each year sell out within minutes. With all the cancellations, how could the annual lighting of the giant Christmas tree in Old Town, which typically draws about 10,000 people each year, go on safely?

"These were not easy decisions, but they were the only decisions the city could make because COVID-19 was still so bad," Ortiz said. "We just kept thinking: How can we help Christmas still be Christmas? How can we help Nob Hill still be Nob Hill? How can we help Old Town be Old Town?" How could city government help Albuquerque be Albuquerque?

After eight months of reimagining events, by the holidays Bree Ortiz and her team were pros at transforming live performances and activities into online productions. They knew how to harness the power of social media, though not every event could be reduced to screen time. They researched how other cities were handling big events during the pandemic, but they found little guidance.

"We were stricter than some cities, so in places with less closures it was just normal stuff," Ortiz said. "But in places as strict as here, staff was just sent home and there was nothing. It turns out we were the only events people in similar cities who still had jobs and were still on the job, and I was so thankful for that." So Ortiz and the other event elves kept brainstorming about how to save Christmas. It came to Ortiz in her restless sleep. Why not, she thought, combine a little River of Lights with a little Twinkle Light Parade?

"I literally thought about it in the middle of the night," Ortiz said. "Had it not been that hour I might have jumped out of bed and started making calls."

She waited for a more reasonable hour to hire thirteen artisans to create holiday light installations, some that incorporated pieces borrowed from the

Twinkle Light, December 19, 2020. Photo by Jessica Roybal, courtesy Albuquerque Museum digital Archives, object #PA2021.032.007

River of Lights display. By December 2020, the installations were ready to be placed in storefronts of participating businesses along Central Avenue in Nob Hill for people to enjoy as they strolled by, or from the comfort and safety of their own vehicles as they cruised Route 66.

In all, forty windows and several parking lots from Carlisle to Washington along Central were illuminated as part of what was dubbed the Route 66 Shop & Glow. Additional holiday light displays were installed in storefronts throughout EDO, East Downtown, which runs west of Nob Hill along Route 66. The project, which glowed through December 2020, brought not only holiday joy but also holiday shoppers, guided by sidewalk message boards that identified shops and restaurants providing carryout and curbside pickup.

Ortiz and the community events team also had an idea about how to save the Old Town tree lighting, by quietly changing the date from the usual first Friday in December to an earlier, less busy Sunday. Changes had already come years before to the tradition of the tree. Henry Aceves, the man who had saved Christmas, was gone.

Ruben Martinez was twelve years old when his Uncle Henry Aceves brought Albuquerque's Christmas tree to Plaza Don Luis in Old Town. Like his other young cousins in the large and tight-knit Aceves and Martinez families, Ruben had grown up with the tree lighting and his relatives' involvement with it. The holiday event wasn't just a city tradition but also a family one. After the lighting, family and invited friends gathered in the

Despite the pandemic, improvements to public spaces and construction projects carried on full tilt. COO Lawrence Rael and Mayor Keller survey the Railyards in 2020, amidst improvements. Photo courtesy Mayor's Office, City of Albuquerque.

Old Town Basket and Rug Shop and adjoining suites for bowls of steaming posole with red chile and tortillas, the specialty of Martinez's aunt, Sharon Wright. Beer and margaritas flowed for the adults. Laughter filled the air.

"It was a tradition we looked forward to every year," said Laura Martinez, longtime general manager of the Old Town Basket and Rug Shop and one of Ruben Martinez's aunts. "The tree has been in our family for three generations now, and that's all thanks to Henry."

Once the state rolled out vaccines in 2021, the City of Albuquerque Environmental Health Department communicated new messages to encourage vaccinations.

In 2013, Aceves' health began to fail after a series of strokes. Each time, he fought his way back, a little weaker in body but not in mind and certainly not at heart. He knew it was time to start passing along the family tradition of the tree for when he was gone. Aceves chose his nephew, Ruben Martinez.

"I guess you could say he was passing the torch to me," said Martinez, then a young man starting his own family. "I became his right-hand man, the muscle man, you could say, dealing mostly with the physical aspects of what it entails to make the tree happen. I was never the boss. That was always Uncle Henry."

In 2017, Henry Aceves' health continued to decline. In October 2017, Aceves passed away peacefully, surrounded by family, as he almost always was. He was sixty-nine, weeks shy of his seventieth birthday. Ruben Martinez was ready to step up to take over the tree duties, supported by the family, including Aceves' two daughters, Ashley and Erin. It was, Martinez said, the honor of his life.

"This is a tree that thousands come to see every year, and to carry on the tradition of something that is so important to the city and so important to my uncle is a responsibility I hold with great respect, not just for myself but for my family, for everybody," Martinez said.

Just as his Uncle Henry had taught him, Ruben Martinez rounded up family members with flatbed trucks a week before Thanksgiving to make the pilgrimage to a tree farm in Rociada, a small village nestled at the foot of the Sangre de Cristo Mountains in northern New Mexico, stopping once along the way for their traditional breakfast at Charlie's Spic and Span Bakery & Cafe in Las Vegas, New Mexico, before returning to Albuquerque by sundown. The hundreds of trees were then deposited at the Aceves' home off Rio Grande Boulevard, and sorted into piles according to height. Family and City of Albuquerque employees constructed the tree, stringing more than 400 strands sparkling with 10,000 LED lights and hanging hundreds of bright red ribbons and glittering snowflakes.

"Uncle Henry downplayed it, but it's a lot of work," Martinez said, chuckling. "He assembled an army of us, and it takes an army. Quality control isn't an issue because it's family. It's a sense of pride."

In 2020, the family was concerned about how COVID-19 and the public health orders would affect the tradition. Martinez and the Aceves sisters called a family meeting to discuss what they should do.

"At the forefront was maintaining the safety of the family and the community and the integrity of the tradition, and how do you do that with social distancing," Martinez said. "We had concerns that this could turn negative if putting together and lighting the tree became a health issue, or looked like it was."

Martinez conferred with Bree Ortiz at Arts & Culture and agreed to quietly light the tree on the earlier date, videotape the lighting, and put it online so the community could still watch it remotely. Martinez and the Aceves sisters also made the tough choice of asking older family members to stay home and not participate in the tree construction and lighting ceremony. Instead a skeleton crew of younger cousins and city employees would do the job. Gone, too, was Aunt Sharon's famous posole and red chile and the big family gathering and reception held after the tree lighting.

"These were hard choices, but they had to be made," Martinez said. "In the end, the tree was lit, the tradition was saved, and we all endured."

Albuquerque had endured, too, through a year that was painful, soul-clutching, and strange. That endurance forced the city to become flexible and creative. 2020 had forced city officials to make the tough decisions, to take the criticism, to rethink, regroup, and push forward.

"As I reflect on 2020, there's no doubt these were unprecedented times from a global pandemic to a powerful fight against racial injustice," Mayor Keller wrote in his holiday greetings to the city. "Facing these challenges revealed even more of the fundamental Albuquerque resilience that we all know so well. The ways we stepped up together for our community through every challenge this year has made me more proud than ever to live here."

On Christmas Day 2020, the state Department of Health reported 1,465 new cases of COVID-19, 428 of those in Bernalillo County. Hospitals were crammed with 774 COVID-19 patients. Thirty-six people, including twelve in Bernalillo County, would not see the new year because the virus took their lives. The alarming numbers were a reminder that the light at the end of the very dark pandemic tunnel was still a long way off even as the city prepared to bid 2020 farewell. But the end was there, visible. Ahead lay 2021 and the availability of vaccines against COVID-19, a new presidential administration, and new challenges for an Albuquerque team that had been battle-tested by a year of pandemic and protests.

At the crossroads, no one could know what lay ahead, how long the pandemic would last, how many more would die, how polarizing and painful things would become, how much worse it would all be. What was known was that Albuquerque is a city that takes pride in its scabs and its scars and its passionate, profound history. In spite of the darkest days, Albuquerque has always endured, bolstered by hard work and by hope.

So like so many before us, we listen, and we learn. We dare to imagine the day the road ahead is clear of coronavirus, and Albuquerque emerges from the darkness and noise imperfect and magical and real.

One Albuquerque, Many Shifts

by Shelle Sanchez, Director, City of Albuquerque
Arts and Culture Department

City government may not sound like the most scintillating topic to folks. But when we dive into what it means to us as residents, and to the people featured throughout this book, we see how powerful it is in our own daily lives. From the streets on which we want to travel safely to work and the grocery store, to the parks where our kids play, to enjoying hot air balloons in the sky or a hot meal for a senior, surprisingly all of it hinges on a well-run city government.

When the pandemic hit, all of the ways that city government shapes our community took on even more meaning. It's not an exaggeration to say that running the city well became, literally, a matter of life and death.

Albuquerque can often feel more like a small town than some of the major metropolises around us like Phoenix or Denver. But the Duke City is by far the largest municipality in our state with twenty-two departments, nearly 6,000 employees, and a billion-dollar budget. Pivoting an agency of that size is no small feat. If you've ever grappled with red tape, you know that government is not known for being nimble. Fortunately, the team running the city was ready heading into that challenging year. They were ready to make huge shifts.

Starting in 2017, Mayor Keller had laid out clear expectations and well-defined priorities with his leadership team. From day one of his administration, Keller expected his appointed cabinet members to adhere to these goals: communicate openly and proactively with the each other and the public; work with focus and urgency; acknowledge problems and find solutions; be attentive to the daily work of city government, while also pursuing big projects and reforms; respect and respond to deadlines; and be ready and willing to adapt quickly.

The administration challenged itself to build on Albuquerque's many strengths, including natural beauty and outdoor spaces; resilient, diverse, and resourceful communities; strong arts, cultural, and creative ecosystem; long-standing research and tech infrastructure; and a connected network of nonprofit partners. All of these expectations set in 2017 and implemented in 2018 and 2019 prepared the team to pivot quickly, lead effectively, maintain and expand city services during the pandemic, and work responsively in 2020 during unprecedented uncertainty.

If you live in Albuquerque, you have probably seen t-shirts or billboards promoting city services with a "One Albuquerque" logo. To the Keller administration, One Albuquerque is much more than just a marketing slogan. It's truly a call to action, asking all of us to step up and face our challenges head on, and to champion our successes together.

A supporting foundation even came to life to support these ideals. A group of bipartisan community leaders took it upon themselves to start the

One Albuquerque Fund (onealbuquerque.org), building on the belief that Albuquerque needs a community-wide effort from individuals who devote time, talent, and even money to help solve deep-rooted problems and invest in impactful solutions. In years past, Albuquerque mayors hosted an annual "Mayor's Ball," an exclusive charity event for people who could afford a high-dollar ticket, and it ultimately generated less than $50,000 for one nonprofit each year. With Keller's support, the One Albuquerque Fund wanted to do better and find a path that could connect philanthropy directly with the city's biggest priorities now and into the future. The original board of Charles Ashley III, Drew Dolan, Bob White, Pilar Westell and Westly Wellborn began expanding fundraising efforts to include more community partners and to tackle specific challenges like affordable housing and public safety recruitment. This new organization, established pre-pandemic, became an impactful partner throughout the challenges of 2020. The One ABQ Fund donated large sums towards emergency housing, medical and healthcare supplies, and more when it mattered most.

At the onset of the pandemic, the Emergency Operations Center (EOC) was quickly at the center of the city government's coordinated response to the public health crisis. The EOC's typically small staff was amplified by members of other departments, who were reassigned to help with the center's increased workload. The EOC spearheaded many pandemic initiatives, such as collecting and disseminating timely data, finding and procuring hand sanitizer and masks, and distributing vaccines. Quickly staffing up the EOC is one example of dozens of shifts city government made to move employees from less busy posts in community centers, special events or libraries, for example, to departments whose work increased during the pandemic.

In April 2020, as the pandemic ramped up, the city's leadership team implemented major cost saving measures while simultaneously tracking pandemic-related expenditures. Although it was unclear to everyone how long this would last, it was obvious that financial disruptions were likely, so it was important to build any savings possible in the spring and early summer–the fourth quarter of the city's fiscal year. To avoid the massive layoffs and furloughs seen in other cities, that first spring of the pandemic every department and division canceled or delayed non-essential contracts, slowed or delayed hiring for vacant positions, and reviewed every single purchase to determine if it was one that could be delayed. Keller's leadership team, several of whom previously worked in the State Auditor's office, also knew immediately that any unanticipated expenses and every reallocation of resources needed to be clearly documented and tracked, including the reassignment of staff to pandemic-related duties, work-at-home status, or stay-at-home status.

During the early uncertainty of the pandemic in the spring of 2020, the administration made intentional and strategic human resource decisions that ensured city employees kept their jobs throughout an extended period of economic volatility, had access to emergency sick leave to care for themselves or for family with COVID-19, and had access to emergency leave to care for children when schools and daycares were closed. As each department reassigned staff or adjusted their reporting, the administration very quickly established time codes to track these changes. Although this may seem like a minor detail, it meant that the administration could effectively generate reports on the number of employees teleworking, the number of employees engaged directly in pandemic-related services, and the number of employees on sick leave as a result of COVID-19. Once federal relief funding arrived to the City of Albuquerque, this coding meant the administration could effectively use relief funding to reimburse the City's general fund for pandemic-related hours and purchases.

With finer details being managed daily, as it became clear that the pandemic was not a month-long pause of regular life, each city department made a plan answering big-picture questions: "What do we have to keep doing? What can we keep doing? How do we organize our work so our employees are safe and people receiving our services are safe?" Each department analyzed which employees could work from home or report remotely, how staffing pods could accommodate quarantining COVID-19 cases, and what other pivots would keep city services running while adjusting to the many pandemic-inspired challenges.

Senior and multi-generational centers across the city had to cancel their regular social, educational, and nutritional programs inside the centers during the pandemic. Their services shifted to amped-up free meal service, pickup and delivery of essentials to the elderly, and ride services to the infirm. City centers also acted as points of delivery for other pandemic related services, such as PPE giveaways, distributions of food and other essentials for low-income and home-bound seniors, and coordination of donations. Although the public was not inside city senior centers, the work of supporting seniors did not slow down, but in fact accelerated.

As the public was reaching out for information about the pandemic, support, and sometimes just connection as stay-at-home orders ensued, the number of phone calls to the Constituent Services Department in the Mayor's office increased manifold, as did calls to its 311 information line operators.

Need was strong everywhere across the city during the pandemic. As the streets were empty, so were the locally-owned and operated businesses that were central to the Keller administration's economic development strategies. During a time of vastly decreased business, city government found a way to provide relief and help to stabilize Albuquerque's small businesses. The City of Albuquerque Department of Economic Development distributed $10 million to small businesses and one thousand business grants during the pandemic to entrepreneurs and arts and culture professionals from federal monies and other sources. The first round of funding went out before the first round of federal relief funds arrived to the City of Albuquerque. The city released a second round of monies to small businesses in the fall of 2021.

In an effort to keep services in place and to keep staff healthy and safe, the Solid Waste Department and many other city departments quickly had employees report to work remotely. Drivers reported to their trucks and clocked in, rather than going inside the building and gathering before shifts. City building inspectors and environmental health inspectors also reported remotely and received work assignments via email rather than reporting to their physical offices first. ABQ BioPark zookeepers and aquarists created split teams so that half of each animal team would report each day, so if one person on a team was COVID positive the entire team could quarantine, and there would still be staff members to care for the animals. Construction permitting, city planners, 311 operators, fiscal teams, human resources professionals, and many more staff quickly made plans to work remotely. City staffers had to ramp up their individual technical skills and adjust their internal and external communications and home offices. Unlike some other governments, the City of Albuquerque's services continued even though many physical office spaces sat empty. This monumental shift in work environment was a heavy lift for the Department of Technology and Innovation, which was charged with quickly providing telecommuting resources and capabilities to thousands of city employees working in home offices. Their myriad considerations included hardware, software, security, troubleshooting, and much more as city employees shifted to telecommuting.

With the drastic shift online, the City of Albuquerque Arts & Culture Department shifted to virtual programming including concerts, gallery walk-throughs, library story times, and more, much of which will remain as people became more accustomed and desirous of online programming during the pandemic. GovernmentTV (GOVTV), one of the City of Albuquerque's public television stations, handled the bulk of the broadcasting workload for real-time communications by airing the mayor's near-daily briefings to the public, city council meetings, and COVID-19 informational messaging. The GOVTV team increased availability of online creative and cultural programming from public libraries, museums, the BioPark, and local creatives through its Local Access Channel and on YouTube. The city's media team also partnered with Albuquerque Public Schools to air daily programming for APS students in the evening after New Mexico PBS aired its programs in the daytime, in order to give families multiple access times for important school content.

Throughout the pandemic, the city's Family and Community Services Department took the lead coordinating COVID-19 wellness hotels. The number of wellness hotels fluctuated based on vacillating needs of the pandemic. Family and Community Services also helped to expand temporary housing and services at the city's Westside Emergency Housing Center, known as the Westside Shelter. Employees from a variety of city departments including Arts & Culture's librarians and special event team staffed the wellness hotels, which provided a range of services, from housing homeless individuals who tested positive for COVID to quarantining first responders who had been exposed to the virus. Family and Community Services provided integral support at all the intersections of running the wellness hotels, providing childcare, rides, and other essential services to the community. Like so many efforts, the wellness hotels alone spawned from incredible partnerships between city government and community partners.

In the spring of 2020, during evolving stay-at-home orders from the state health department, Mayor Keller and his leadership team decided to bolster construction projects, seeing this time as an opportunity to finish existing construction, start new construction, and push a large number of road work projects while the streets were largely empty. City construction projects, which could be done largely outside in a COVID-safe manner, increased during the pandemic in Albuquerque, providing crucial income, jobs, and public infrastructure improvements during shutdowns.

By early summer 2020, the leadership team increased their focus on the city's strengths, including great weather, access to nature, public open spaces, and local economy. The Planning Department, Metropolitan Redevelopment Agency, and Fire Marshal's Office coordinated efforts to quickly update ordinances and adjust permitting rules so that restaurants could easily expand outdoor seating on sidewalks and other public spaces during the pandemic. This move was an impactful and natural adjustment, given Albuquerque's warm weather, which quickly increased small business revenues and encouraged pandemic-healthy seating. Increased outdoor dining was one of many pandemic pivots that has remained as people will be able to choose patio and sidewalk seating year-round regardless of public health orders. Keller's team also prioritized reopening (and keeping open) public outdoor spaces during the pandemic, which required ongoing dialogue with the governor and state health department, to ensure Albuquerque's walking trails, bike trails, open spaces, parks, BioPark, and the beloved Tingley Beach all remained healthy extracurricular options during extended periods of social isolation.

The pandemic's shift of needs and social and physical isolation were not the only difficult crisis of 2020 in Albuquerque. The sculpture *La Jornada* is a part of the City of Albuquerque's permanent public art collection and has inspired discussion and disagreement since its inception decades ago. Installed on the grounds of the Albuquerque Museum, the multi-figure art installation is not managed by the museum or part of its collection, but rather part of the City of Albuquerque's Public Art collection. For those interested in *La Jornada*, files and information about it can be accessed on the City of Albuquerque's Arts & Culture Department website under the Race, History and Healing project.

In the fall of 2020, the City of Albuquerque was forced to do another hard shutdown of public spaces and public offices that had reopened in August and September. In some ways, this was easier to do again after months of adjustments to services; however, at this point, public servants were exhausted like the rest of the community, and also like the rest of the community, more of them had COVID or had recovered from the virus.

Everything seemed to peak in difficulty months into the pandemic and right before the holiday season. Mayor Keller continued to rely on regular and direct communications to the public and city-wide planning with department directors and public health experts to push through the final shutdown of 2020. Just as they did earlier in the year, the plans and pivots were shared openly with the public so the community knew how their local government was responding.

As soon as the production of COVID-19 vaccines was announced, the City of Albuquerque began making plans to acquire and distribute vaccines in partnership with the State of New Mexico Department of Health. This was an exciting step forward and also another challenge of coordination and prioritization for Keller's administration. For its own employees, the administration planned to quickly make the vaccine available to the frontline workers like police officers and firefighters who interact closely with others. Knowing the vaccine would later become available to the general public, the administration planned to prioritize equity in vaccine distribution, making sure that where residents live or what language they speak would not become a barrier to access. Even though the development of the vaccine seemed to mark an end to many of the pandemic's biggest challenges, it also coincided with the unforeseen challenges and big opportunities that came with what many expected to be the return to a "new normal." As 2020 came to a close, city leaders were looking forward to turning the page on a difficult year and returning to projects and initiatives that had been sidelined by the crisis. As we know now, however, the end of 2020 did not mean the crisis was over.

This book is a snapshot in time: the year 2020. But at the time of its completion two years later, communities around the globe are still grappling with pandemic-related challenges. In the "before time," some governments seemed slow and unwieldy in responding to the communities they serve. But these hefty and varied shifts undertaken by the City of Albuquerque demonstrate how a crisis can spur immediate action. All the way up and down the city's organizational chart, its leaders and frontline workers didn't step aside—they stepped up. They designed each of these decisions, each of these real-time pivots, to save lives and save livelihoods. During the pandemic, the mission became crystal clear—get Albuquerque through COVID-19 stronger than ever, hand-in-hand with residents. This was a time where City Hall and city residents were more interconnected than ever. We each had a role to play, and we can be proud of how Albuquerque handled the greatest crisis of our times.

Kimo, May 7, 2021. Photo by Nathaniel Tetsuro Paolinelli, courtesy Albuquerque Museum Digital Archives, object #PA2021.034.005

"Hometown Heroes" mural. Photo courtesy Albuquerque Museum.

AFTERWORD

**by Sarita Nair, City of Albuquerque Chief Administrative Officer 2017-2022
January 2022, Albuquerque, New Mexico**

Five hundred days after March 10, 2020, the City of Albuquerque's public art team unveiled *Lost and Found, Art and Stories from the Pandemic*. To participate in the project, anyone could tell the story of something they lost or found during the COVID shutdown and the months that followed.

I told the interviewer that I found time. They laughed because so many other people had said they lost a year. Now looking back, maybe both things are true. Time got weird.

In the early days of the pandemic, time moved very slowly. The hours were longer than usual as we evaluated each department, employee-by-employee, and figured out how to close city offices while still providing services.

Longer still were the hours between a COVID exposure and a test result. An hour of uninterrupted sleep felt like a luxurious weekend. Twenty-hour workdays were the "new normal." Sometimes I learned a year's worth of lessons in a day—about everything from communicable diseases, to contested cultural history, to macroeconomics.

In some moments, time stopped during the pandemic: the moment I was asked how we should prepare for a nationwide body bag shortage. The moment we smelled smoke and a fire alarm went off in City Hall, and I thought, we can't possibly have this happen now, too. The moment preceding the verdict in the Derek Chauvin trial, filled with anxiety and dread, and the moment after the judge read the word "guilty," with its mix of relief and sorrow and anger.

Time became silly putty during the pandemic—messy, elastic, distorted. The days were slow, but the months were fast. The now nineteen months and counting of the pandemic were some of the longest days and shortest months of my life.

In this time warp, it feels strange to write an afterword because the idea of "after" is complex. I am not writing this after the pandemic. In fact, in New Mexico on the very day I write this (October 30, 2021), ten people died of COVID and another 1,054 positive cases were confirmed.

Reliving 2020 through the lens of Joline's powerful storytelling helped me understand what "after" could mean. Her work reveals the order that lay under the chaos of 2020. She found patterns and cycles that one can only see with distance. Albuquerque after 2020, although not "post-pandemic," is definitely a different place.

Or maybe, like in the spiral pictograph, Albuquerque is the same place but we are different. Enough time has passed after 2020 that we can see some of how this time changed us, and the lessons that we will take through the rest of our work and our lives.

Lesson One: Love and compassion are the center of good policy.

At one point in the pandemic I said to twenty or so exhausted young staff members, "If you're not crying at least once a week, you're probably doing it wrong." The tears of 2020 were from sadness, exhaustion, frustration, overwork, and grief. Love and compassion were the only things that kept us all going. Whether it was opening wellness hotels for the most vulnerable families, feeding seniors, supporting businesses, or talking to our own employees, compassion had to be at the center of everything we did in city government during the pandemic. When childcare workers and bus drivers and zookeepers were pushed to their limits, it was their love for the work and the community that brought them back to face another day. Especially as the anger in our society seems to grow stronger and stronger, we need to keep love and compassion at the center of our work. We've learned that there is no other way to tackle the tremendous challenges Albuquerque still has ahead.

Lesson Two: When a moment and a movement converge, we must seize the opportunity to make big changes.

The Black Lives Matter movement was not new in 2020. We had all seen videos of police brutality before. Maybe the difference was that many of us were watching that officer take the life of George Floyd from the isolation of a lockdown where nobody felt safe to breathe the air around them. Maybe we had more empathy, or maybe we had more anger that needed a channel. In any case, the fickle momentum of the general public got behind the Black Lives Matter movement in mid-2020. This created a space where it felt like we could take a big swing. Projects that we had been nudging along cautiously went from seeming too controversial to seeming too small. For Albuquerque, seizing this moment meant two major moves. First, we gathered the political courage to drastically reimagine first response and to decriminalize poverty and trauma by forming the Albuquerque Community Safety Department (ACS).

With its first two cohorts of behavioral health responders now taking hundreds of calls, ACS is on the path to create the fundamental systemic change that we hoped it would.

Secondly, we took a leap in our ongoing work to direct resources to historically neglected groups, by helping to form the Black Community Investment Fund. The $1 million that city government seeded into that fund is already making a difference for businesses and nonprofits, even as the community's larger, long-term vision comes together. I am deeply grateful that the people's courage to protest and speak out created an opportunity to make big changes.

Lesson Three: We can do things faster than we thought we could.

We turned $300 million-plus of capital into construction projects, roads, and jobs in eighteen months. We cut the hiring time for city employees by over 60%. We revamped our design and building processes. The sense of urgency may ebb and flow, but the capabilities that evolved during 2020 are here to stay. With the federal government pouring billions of dollars into infrastructure, technology, and social programs, we are going to need every ounce of innovation and nimbleness to make sure Albuquerque is not left behind in the recovery post-pandemic.

Lesson Four: We are swimming in the river of history, and we can't be afraid of the undertow.

As Confederate statues toppled across the country, we knew that it didn't matter how different Albuquerque's story was—change was coming. After the violence and removal of the Oñate statue, our leadership team managed to balance taking responsibility for the city's role and making space for many different voices. The city's Race, History and Healing Project was just the beginning. In 2021, as an international conversation about gravesites of Indigenous people arose, a sign that commemorated a burial site in the middle of Albuquerque was stolen. Rather than shrinking from difficult conversations, we moved toward them. We engaged our Commission on American Indian and Alaska Native Affairs and our liaisons to Native communities, and took their lead on how to address the signs and the site. These conversations are going to become more common over time. Divergent narratives about what is happening at this very moment are all around us. The ability to reconcile and find a path through those stories is a skill we need to keep at the ready.

Lesson Five: We need to build a foundation strong enough to hold a house we can't yet imagine.

In December 2017, Mayor Keller brought the One Albuquerque vision with him to City Hall. It was our motto and the blueprint of how we ran local government. We knew that breaking down silos would make government work better, but we had no idea that cooperation was about to become a matter of life and death. We built an Office of Equity and Inclusion and an Office of Civil Rights within our first year because Albuquerque needed them. We never dreamt that these would be the teams reaching out to protestors, managing the demands of asylum seekers, and developing new trainings for police. In 2018, when we revamped the 3-1-1 city information number and started monitoring its data, we didn't know large item trash pickups would increase by 3000% in 2020 as people sat at home amid too much stuff. Those continuity of operations plans that the Office of Emergency Management pleaded and pushed us to complete in 2019—we never thought we would use them to run city government.

As Kurt Vonnegut wrote, "History is only a list of surprises. It can only prepare us to be surprised yet again." The truth is, you don't know what you are building a team to handle. You build it as strong as possible, align it closely with your values, and hope it can withstand whatever comes your way.

So the question I find myself asking here in "the after" is: how is this actually "the before"? What do we need to build today for tomorrow's surprises? What are the vulnerabilities that the next crisis will magnify? How do we fortify our team so they can continue to lead at this remarkably high level without burning out?

As Joline so poignantly captures, in February 2020, we didn't know that we were living in the time before the pandemic. We also didn't know we were living in the time before the largest public works funding programs in our nation's history would enable us to take on big, bold projects. Now that we know just how uncertain the future can be, our work is to use our imaginations and our love for the city to prepare Albuquerque for whatever we may encounter.

Epilogue
Lost & Found
Art & Stories from the Pandemic

In late 2020, Mayor Keller asked the Department of Arts & Culture to find a creative and meaningful way to honor the great loss experienced from the pandemic that would also lift up the resiliency of our city and its residents. The collaborative art exhibit, *Lost & Found*, invited the Albuquerque community to reflect and share stories of loss and learning from the many months of the pandemic—and especially their experiences in 2020. The Department of Arts & Culture launched *Lost & Found* in 2021 with a temporary public art installation on Civic Plaza, featuring more than 500 black-and-white paper flags designed by nine local artists representing the loss, hope, challenges, victories, and mixed emotions of the pandemic. Community members visited the installation and shared their own stories of loss and discovery through conversation.

Lost & Found resonated, and more people wanted to share. Stations were set up at the KiMo Theater during ArtWalk. Then sessions were scheduled at senior centers, community centers, and with school groups. The *Lost & Found* team set out to collect 550 stories, and got more than 1400. The stories are now online, on paper, and some are part of a video performance; many are part of a poetic collage on the pages that follow.

Dozens of individuals, poets, performers, and city employees contributed significantly to *Lost & Found*. Many thanks to the City of Albuquerque Public Art team, who invited artists and then made the first installation on Civic Plaza a beautiful space for reflecting and gathering. Thank you to the visual artists Lauren Smith, Diane Pallet, Bette Yozell, Celine Gordon, Jakia Fuller, Emma Eckert, Kate Coucke, Manuel Hernandez, and Susan Roden, whose art brought beauty and energy to the installation that radiated beyond Civic Plaza. Thanks to the story team of Diana Delgado, Katie Farmin, Rhiannon Frazier, and Madrone Matysiak (plus many more creatives and youth artists that helped along the way). Thank you to all the community members who took the time to write and share their stories, reminding us how connected and resilient we are. Thank you for all of your efforts along the way and for believing deeply that everyone's story is beautiful and deserves a moment of heartfelt listening.

THANKS FOR SINGING TO ME, IF ONLY FOR A SECOND

a poetic collage of the words from citizens of Albuquerque through the Lost and Found project, curated and arranged by EKCO poets Tanesia Hale Jones, Valerie Martínez, Elsa Menendez, Michelle Otero, and Shelle Sanchez.

There's a Virus

Overseas there's a virus.
Mom, are we going to quarantine?
M'ija! Don't worry. I bought everything.
It's only in China.

It's spreading.
It's everywhere.
It's here.

Everything feels slow, and long, and quiet.

I lost my band
I lost my friend
Lost physical closeness
Live music

My life was paper. Flat and dry. Brittle.
And tears would tear it apart.

I lost my house.
I lost my job.
I closed my business.
People bought all the toilet paper!
It was odd but that is what we had to deal with.

Something came to me and said,
Don't worry about it, just take care of Mom.
So we started quarantining.
Calm. Taking precautions.

I lost my wits
I lost some teeth
I lost direction

Hello to the reader that's reading my words.
Hello to the listener who's hearing my voice.

So I tried baking sourdough.
I made a collage of all the things in my house,
everything the color orange.
I watched and watched and watched the Tiger King.
I started making music as a way
to vent my feelings into something.

It was my freshman year. The thought of an early spring break
made me rejoice. Abundance!

Little did we know the normality of our world,
our days, our lives would be lost.
Now life is torn up, shredded, mud with water,
strained into flat rectangles.

You missed my birthday
I missed your birthday
An anniversary.

Grandma in a nursing home.
My uncle gasping for breath on the other end of the phone.
The beginning of the plague.
Paper life. Thin, transparent paper.

Sometimes I call myself a failure, lazy, sometimes alive.
Overseas, there's a virus.

The future holds secrets, mysteries–
–all ground down and stripped bare,
under silk and stone nothing–
–maybe they were always there.

More Than 550 Days

It's been more than five hundred and fifty days
Since it all began–
Since I felt the heartbeat of a bass drum–
Since I felt longing,
Since I last saw your face.

Desde un principio,
Desde que volví a nacer.

It's been 550 days since I felt normal,
traveled to the Pacific. went to the beach, since the moon set.

More than 550 days
since I felt someone else's heartbeat,
things were normal,
the start of something new.

550 days
since I've seen my kids,
heard my grandpa's voice,
had a drink–

–Since we all traveled together–
–So many days since the world changed.

There's nowhere else to go.
550 days since I wasn't worried about death.

Call me Triste
Call me Lonely
It's been 550 days since I've been held.

I wait for you to notice the bad things happening
and offer me support. I wait for you to call me,
but you stopped doing it.

A kiss on the mouth?

It seems so close,
like it's just about, almost–
–on the edge of the future.

School Daze

I enjoy a lot of time to myself. I was okay being away from my friends for a few months. When it was time to quarantine and do online school, I thought it was pretty fun at first. But then spending so much time away from my friends made me pretty miserable.

A lotta people I know got COVID. So, that sucked.
I wasn't a kid with good grades, and didn't have any intention of trying.

We got sent home freshman year because of an outbreak.
Now, we're Juniors, wearing masks.
I can't even remember people's faces.

My sister drilled in me the importance of a good G.P.A.,
even during a pandemic. I barely passed. I just cannot learn online, pay attention online, cannot laugh online, cannot still be online.

It feels like I am always, always on standby.
I'm offline.
Can I find myself in the memory on my hard drive?

The pandemic doesn't quit learning!

So I left the house, gave my heart to the pavement, mapped the neighborhood with my feet. Learned the names of dogs behind their fences. It's how I broke my nose, my art, my tooth.

It's like being in a car, that's on a train, that's falling off a cliff.

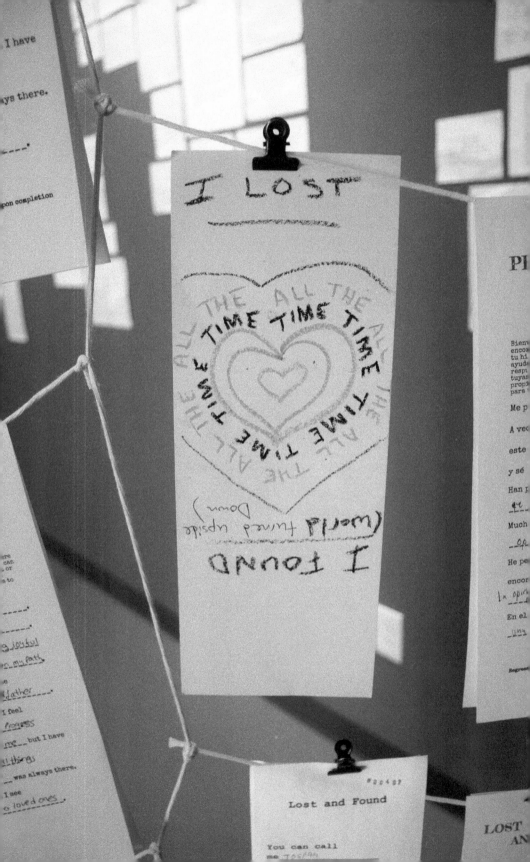

Hands Drawing Themselves Out of Boredom

Everything just feels slow, and long, and quiet.
Hands drawing themselves out of boredom.
A place where I think I can think.

Medicinal herbs growing in the yard.
Dandelions exploding from sidewalks.

All these cars and bicycles locked up
in my apartment complex.

I've lost my taste, my desire to taste.

I wish I could find someone
to come with me to eat Indian food.
Will anyone come with me?

People gone, community gone,
everything locked away.

Even before the virus, the system
was not set up for me.
Protests, political divisions, forests burning.
Plaid on stripes on scribbles.

Maybe some things I've forgotten are meant to be forgotten?
Maybe some of what I've lost is better for being lost?

I've started making rye bread, now, with cocoa powder.
I've started a new book.
I cleaned out those junk drawers.

I feel guilty, but can I say it? I feel liberated!
Alive, in my feelings

Closer to my best friend
72
At peace
Happy
Discovering myself

Rebuilding
Not lost
10 years old

Hopeful
Satisfied
One with the sad, whole world

Secure
74 and old as a giant turtle.
Writing, and I really know why
OK, I'm trying to figure it out.

You can call me Amy or Terra or Stacy or Jasmine or Chris.
Me puedes llamar Carlos, Maria, Esperanza, Kane, Otilia, Juan.

I am 28 years old and I finally set off to be on my own.
My eyes are open.

I made it. I barely made it. And now
I'm in a good situation and a good mindset.
Thank you, Ancestors,
for bringing me here.

At least it's not superficial. At least it's not stupid,
No matter how hard.

I went looking for what I lost but found something unexpected–
sharing a meal, sharing a trip, just hanging out.

When I got my vaccine, I cried with joy, hope, love.
Now, I don't take it for granted, anything,
no matter how hard.

The Slippery Mechanism of Who Knows What

My mental health started to decline around August 2020.
Time passed and, oh, it got worse.

Sophomore year was my worst year of school ever.
Online school? I didn't like it at all and it was just hard for me.
I didn't even pass enough classes; I was too depressed to care.

The weirdest thing is that no one in my family got sick
but it didn't seem to make things any better.

My bathroom, now labeled as the quarantine bathroom,
was the place for anyone who tested positive,

so I had to use my parents' bathroom or the one downstairs.
Sometimes I had to hold it so hard the tears came,
and I was raging.

Summer 2020, my sister drilled in me the importance
of having a good G.P.A. I was miserable halfway through
my freshman year and then when we shut down.

I remember thinking just two more weeks and things will go back to
"normal."
Those two weeks passed and two more and two more and two more, and
I found myself confused at the state of the world. I didn't understand
what was happening and didn't know if we had any control over any of it.

I lost
I lost
I lost my
I lost my past
Lost creativity
Lost my social side, my confidence to talk to new people.
A grandfather and an estranged grandmother.

I lost motivation, lost passion, the feeling of being stable.
I lost my keys, like 500 times!

I lost out on love. I lost my hope, my face
and so many of my teenage years.
The isolation is what gets you.

Our specific losses collide
with the slippery mechanism
of who knows what.

Who knows what.
What I need? A life trajectory.
Tiny ways I can learn to set myself free:

Maybe walks, dear to my heart piano songs,
The refreshing taste of snow.
Animals.
At least animals know how to take care of each other.

I learned to treasure all kinds of things:
Baseball
Going to McDonald's

Patience
Truth
Trust
Going to places with no mask
People that used to bug the hell out of me
Halloween with or without a mask

Being dragged along for grocery shopping
Going to actual school
I guess I've learned a few things

A year ago I was shy; right now I am funny.
My smile was always there.
My dog is always there.

Sometimes I call myself an armadillo
Sometimes I call myself a ringer
Sometimes I call myself the snake, in flux, nothing.

In-person school? Not that bad after all.

I think the future holds happiness.
I think the future holds beautiful skies.

I think the future is a mug of hot tea and old photos.

Is there a bright side?

After restrictions lifted a little, my uncle and auntie
started coming over every weekend and they would stay
'til late at night playing cards and watching TV.
It was fun.

Mystery was always there.
I guess I've learned a few things.
Community was always there.

Sometimes You Just Have to Escape

My mom had to walk away from her job to keep me safe.
In this way, she sang for us.
She revealed herself, one story at a time,
finally exploding from the page
even as life slowed around us–
–spilling into the next frame
like a bloom and a frenzy.

I started to dream.
A superhero appeared.
Zodiac Girl!

Sometimes you just have to escape to some other world.

It began with her origins,
out of the ordinary,
see-sawing and acrobatic,
nothing you could predict.
Twists and turns.

I lost
I lost my
I lost my past
I lost my mind
I lost my creativity
COVID took my grandfather and an estranged grandmother.

I really was suicidal
I hate how scared I feel how when what I love
can be gone just like that.

I lost my wits
I lost some teeth
I lost courage
I lost direction
I cry in my car after trips to the grocery store.
The end is near!

Ears to the ground,
she also hears:

You can call me Mandy, Lorenzo, Michelle,
Grizz, Dawn, Swish, Elizabeth, Kia, Monica,

Anytime Waving Mario,
Sometimes I call myself Rainbow.

Rodrigo, Too Worried, Sophia, Barbara,
Z, Joe, Isaiah, Bill, Ashley, Tiny, Aiden, Amy

You can call me Human.
Call back to me. Call me
a name I will recognize
I'm trying to fix this light.
Hay la posibilidad de tiempo mejor.
Un dedal lleno de esperanza.
Un sol muy brillante.

And Zodiac, she says:
these stories–I carry them with me,
deep in my gut.
I spring forward into action
Powered by your words.

I think the future holds something good.
One year ago I was 7, right now I am 8.
Birds, blue-winged rivers, robots that fly,
I can see it, someday, the end of the pandemic.

I think the future holds unicorns.
I think the future holds the sea.
Mystery was always there.
Mama was always there.
Community was always there.

And Love, I believe Love
was always there.

Call me a story, or call me hope.
Call me whenever you want.
I have a new set of communication skills.
I am loved enough to know how lucky I am.

Here's one good thing: I lost my butt.

New opportunities for fellowship will emerge.
And puppies!
Things will get better not a ton, but enough.

And now I think I've finally got enough courage to say:
I don't want to go to your pool party!

Stories have skins, lives unfolding. They learn to learn
all Beauty, Hope, Moon, Sky, sun, and stars.
My daughter my soul my sister

Perdi quizas los anhelos
O esperanzas y sueños
Que tenia, pero me
Encontré con las piernas más.

Thank you for holding your body on the line
right up against the breath.

We are in this together,
haciendo rompecabezas,
poniendo limites.

Roll up the ball of dark and loss
and hope and courage and mighty thighs
and send it flying toward the future!

Lose yourself.
Walk to the River.
Go in circles, exhausted, exuberant.

Fall into the current.
Join me on this side of the dark.
Lift each other out.

Lose yourself.
Find a different version.
Open to the wonder
And then call back to me.

And if you have the choice: to walk
on 30 feet of straight-up barbed wire
or go through 14 months of isolation again,
say you will walk up the barbed wire.

Say it.
And she will recognize your name.

My Sister Asked Me to Tell You This

It's been 550 days since I was at daycare and a lady brought in her pet turtle. She told us not to touch it, not to pick it up. I picked it up and kissed it. The turtle latched onto my lip and it took two people to get it off.

Most days I felt like a performance art piece for one.
I never wanted to leave my corner of the world.

A litany of embarrassing Zoom moments:

I farted super-loud and realized I wasn't muted.
Camera off, I belted Billie Eilish and realized I hadn't hit "Mute".
My cat showed her butthole to my boss.

Hosting a meeting with 50 people. My husband didn't realize the door was open to my office when he got out of the shower. I rearranged my desk.
I never got dressed.

I was thinking when no one could find any toilet paper,
where's the Sears catalog when you need it?

I laugh, but I have forgotten comfort,
ease, little places of freedom.

I have forgotten what it feels like to hug my friend Ezra.

Early days at the emergency center.
A worldwide shortage of body bags and freezers.

I can't keep the images, and I can't keep them from coming.

I got COVID even with three shots. I went to the emergency room
and they told me to quarantine 2 weeks. I quarantined 3 weeks.
I sprayed Lysol everywhere.

Where are my thoughts, my spirituality, my peace?

My daughter, a nurse at UNM, would come home, take off all her clothes in the garage while we all went to our rooms, put on a bathrobe, go straight to her bedroom where her husband delivered her meals. For months.

I'm like a prisoner. My son wouldn't let me go anywhere, insisted on grocery shopping. The hours we're here together I love him, but I need alone time sometimes!

I have forgotten what it feels like to hug my friend Ezra.

I turned my work into an emergency homeless shelter for women over 65.
Our gym was now where people slept, cots lined up, pillows passed out.
The hardest part was masking my emotions. I had to be a rock.
After awhile, I didn't know how not to be the rock anymore.

I had to keep working at Walmart during the pandemic.
The shelves went from full to empty in three days.
It was like Black Friday every single day.
I had heart surgery 3 months ago. I think it was the pandemic stress.

Vive mi padre en un país sin vacunas.
Y aquí se desperdician.
Les pagan y les rogan que se vacunen.

My daughter gave me a journal, said,
Write down all your recipes. Tamales are the most important.
Did she think I wouldn't be around?

My dog liked me working from home.
My wife? She did not.

For me, last year was real good because
I had two beautiful granddaughters.
Beautiful baby girls.
What a time we live in.

I catalog my days, time with myself and thoughts.
I write them out on the fabric of my humanness.

My Resilience, Our Resilience

Thank you for holding your body
on the line right up against the breath.

We are in it together
haciendo rompecabezas,
poniendo limites.

All beauty, hope, moon, sky, sun, and stars.
Life unfolding.

Stories have skins, they learn to learn.

Perdi quizas los anhelos
O esperanzas y sueños
Que tenia, pero me Encontré
con las piernas más firmes sobre la tierra

I walk to the River today.
Lift me up, join me on this side.
Call me The Wonder

Tyler, Court, daughter, wife, boss, listener,
sister, mom, friendly, Judy

I know my life is love.
I know my stuff.

I am out on a limb, trying to fix this light.
I lay down my stories. I remember
how to stare into the water until it talks.

I walk to the river
I walk to the mountain.

Can we say this isn't much of a story?
More a catharsis, for me.
Beads on a necklace.
Squares on a quilt undone in the pandemic.
I can love so deeply when I'm heard and when I'm seen.

I'm Trying to Fix This Light

These days I call myself

Manny, Spooky Boy, Meccho, Joey,
Solongo, Swish30, Kaia, Monica

Daughter, sister, BFF
Mother, unknown, drama

Call my cell
Call me free will
Jewel, Andres Addison, Sun

Sometimes I call myself athletic
Kind Anita's son
Lazy and silly
I call myself Happy
Call myself Dumb
Call the place where no one speaks
For God's sake please just call

What I've found:
Time.
My mind and new power supply
Love.
The silver lining in the clouds.
My career, new experiences, my dad,
and school and school and school.
A kitten and I got to name it myself–Coco.
Toilet paper!

I can love so deeply when you see me.
We talk grief like recovery–
half a million souls, and counting.
Can we please pause just for a second?

Yes, it's okay.

Me puedes llamar Aaron, Hector, Tabith, Sofia, Suzy, Ray, Ellis, Ryder,
Odelia, Tyriana, Ameriss, Quintyn, Malyk, Angel, Jenna, Andy, Jesus

Beads on a necklace
Squares on a quilt undone in the pandemic

Sometimes I call myself Queen
Sometimes I call myself into the dark
Sometimes I call myself worthless
Sometimes I call myself dangerous
Sometimes I call myself Daddy-o and unemployed

I am living the same day over and over
in my room eyes glued to a screen.

And so I will rearrange the furniture, go to the park,
do homework, run, take a walk, throw a football,
play basketball with my brother, try new food
or drive and drive and drive.
Until I lose my way, on purpose, and find the way back.

And I know the world is large and things will be okay
I believe it will pass or I will endure it.

Like some serious heavy bass.
I know I know a lot more about life and loss and grief.
I'm not naive; I'm a little less stupid.

I wrap my arms around myself
and honor the sky, mirror of the world.

I try to look into its long, dark, silvery eyes.
It's heavy, but it's free.

And I remember to go out to a lake
or at least stare into water,
even in a drain or a drop or a cup.

And I thank it for singing to me–
–more real, more full, more hard, more human–
–if only for a second.

ACKNOWLEDGMENTS

We are grateful for generous photo help and permissions from John Bulten at East Central Ministries, Jami Seymore at KRQE-TV, Danielle Silva at the Mayor's Office, and Jill Hartke, Andrew Rodgers, and Cynthia Garcia at the Albuquerque Museum. Thanks to designer extraordinaire Robin Hesse for her imminent patience. Thanks to Steve Fitzer at the One Albuquerque Fund for copublishing support. Claudia Gallardo De Campbell at the Mayor's Office helped with scheduling interviews, as did Doug Small with the First Lady's Office and William Burleigh with Sarita Nair's office, among others. Thanks to everyone who helped with logistics.

Many thanks to the book project team: Amanda Sutton, book project manager, for her publishing expertise, sagely advice, smart editing, sustaining support and enduring patience; and CABQ Arts & Culture team members Dr. Shelle Sanchez and Hakim Bellamy for recognizing the importance of documenting local history and government; Thanks also to Karl Ortiz, who assisted in procuring ISBNs and copyright; and Tanya Lenti, our pro on promotion, also in the Arts & Culture Department. Many thanks to Justine Freeman for helping get the book over the finish line.

Thank you to all the families who shared their stories with us, and especially the Plath family. Finally, many thanks to the city leaders and workers who provided ongoing service to Albuquerque residents during the pandemic and who made themselves available for interviews for the book.

State of New Mexico

Michelle Lujan Grisham
Governor

EXECUTIVE ORDER 2020-004

**ORDER DECLARING A STATE OF PUBLIC HEALTH EMERGENCY AND
INVOKING THE POWERS PROVIDED BY THE ALL HAZARD EMERGENCY
MANAGEMENT ACT AND THE EMERGENCY LICENSING ACT**

On December 31, 2019, several cases of pneumonia with an unknown cause were detected in Wuhan City, Hubei Province, China and reported to the World Health Organization. The underlying virus giving rise to those reported instances of respiratory illness was later identified as a novel coronavirus disease named COVID-19.

Since it was first identified and reported, COVID-19 has spread globally. Over 100 countries have confirmed cases of COVID-19 and more than 100,000 people have been infected.

The incidence of COVID-19 within the United States has similarly increased. The first domestic report of COVID-19 occurred on January 21, 2020, in Washington State. To date, there have been more than 1,000 reported domestic cases of COVID-19 in 39 states.

Several public health organizations have implemented emergency measures intended to slow the spread of the disease. For example, on January 20, 2020, the United States Centers for Disease Control and Prevention activated its Emergency Operations Center in response to the COVID-19 outbreak. The WHO similarly declared a Public Health Emergency of International Concern shortly thereafter. At least twelve of our sister states, including California, Colorado, Florida, Kentucky, Maryland, Massachusetts, New Jersey, New York, North Carolina, Oregon,

State Capitol • Room 400 • Santa Fe, New Mexico 87501 • 505-476-2200

Utah, and Washington, have also implemented emergency protocols intended to mitigate the transmission of COVID-19.

My administration has been proactive in its approach to the COVID-19 epidemic. Over the last several weeks, I have been in direct and frequent contact with officials overseeing the federal response to the COVID-19 outbreak. Further, my office has worked with the New Mexico Secretary of Health and other State emergency services to develop plans to provide a swift and effective response when the inevitability of COVID-19 in New Mexico ultimately materialized.

On March 11, 2020, the first confirmed cases of COVID-19 were reported in New Mexico. For this reason, it is necessary for all branches of State government to take immediate action to minimize the spread of COVID-19 and to minimize the attendant physical and economic harms.

THEREFORE, for the reasons addressed above, I, Michelle Lujan Grisham, Governor of the State of New Mexico, by virtue of the authority vested in me by the Constitution and the laws of the State of New Mexico, do hereby ORDER and DIRECT:

1.   I hereby invoke and exercise all powers vested in my office under the All Hazard Emergency Management Act, NMSA 1978, §§ 12-10-1 through 12-10-10. All branches of State government shall cooperate with federal authorities, other states, and private agencies to provide resources and services necessary to minimize physical and economic harm and assist in the provision of lodging, shelter, health care, food, transportation, or shipping necessary to protect lives or public property. Further, all political subdivisions within New Mexico shall adhere to Section 12-10-10, which mandates compliance with and enforcement of this Order.

2.   I further proclaim a public health emergency in accordance with NMSA 1978, 12-10A-5 of the Public Health Emergency Response Act. This proclamation is necessary to minimize the spread and adverse impacts of the COVID-19 in our State. All political subdivisions and

Executive Order 2020-004   *Page 2*
State Capitol   •   Room 400   •   Santa Fe, New Mexico 87501   •   505-476-2200   •   fax: 505-476-2226

City at the Crossroads   **197**

geographic areas within the State of New Mexico are affected by the COVID-19 outbreak and, to the extent permitted by law, they are subject to the provisions of this Order. The temporal scope of this emergency is for a period of 30 days and shall remain in effect until further notice. If necessary, after consultation with the Department of Health Secretary, this Order will be renewed and extended. See NMSA 1978, § 12-10A-5 (2003). All public health officials, including those employed by the Department of Health, Human Services Department, and Aging and Long-Term Service Department, are required to assist in the implementation of this Order.

3.   The Department of Health and the Department of Homeland Security and Emergency Management shall collaborate to provide an effective and coordinated response to this public health emergency and shall consult with my office regarding all matters germane to this Order.

4.   All cabinets, departments, and agencies shall comply with the directives in this Order and any instruction given by the Department of Health.

5.   Pursuant to NMSA 1978, § 13-1-127 (2019), I direct the General Services Department Secretary and the Department of Finance and Administration to assist in the emergency purchase of all goods and services necessary to contain, respond, and mitigate the spread of COVID-19 in New Mexico.

6.   The Department of Health and the Department of Homeland Security and Emergency Management shall credential out-of-state professionals who can render aid and necessary services during the pendency of this Order. NMSA 1978, §§ 12-10-10.1 through 12-10-13. (2007).

7.   The Office of the Superintendent of Insurance shall promulgate emergency regulations maximizing the available insurance coverage for New Mexicans suffering from

COVID-19, pneumonia, or influenza, while simultaneously ensuring that medical costs do not create barriers to testing and treatment.

8. The Secretary of the New Mexico Department of Workforce Solutions shall adopt such emergency rules, regulations, or declarations as necessary to ensure that individuals who are experiencing a temporary lay-off or furlough status due to forced absences from work because of COVID-19 are eligible to receive unemployment benefits. I direct the Department of Workforce Solutions Secretary to promulgate emergency rules allowing temporary waivers of claims requirements for affected individuals under NMSA 1978, Section 51-1-5(A)(2) & (3) and any other relevant provisions of law. The emergency waiver provisions should be similar to those already provided by 11.3.300.320(E) & (F) NMAC.

9. I direct the Adjutant General to order into service any elements of the New Mexico National Guard that may be needed to support to civil authorities in response to this public emergency. Such assistance shall be provided during the pendency of this Order at the discretion of the Governor. NMSA 1978, §§ 20-1-1 through 20-1-8; NMSA 1978, §§ 20-4-1- through 20-4-14.

10. In accordance with NMSA 1978, §§ 12-11-23 through 12-11-25 and § 12-10-4(B)(3), the Department of Finance and Administration shall make available emergency financial resources on a continuing basis as necessary to address this emergency to the Department of Health. NMSA 1978, § 12-11-25 (2005). The funds shall be expended to protect the public health, safety, and welfare; to provide those resources and services necessary to avoid or minimize economic or physical harm on a temporary, emergency basis. The funds shall be paid out only in an amount specified by warrants drawn by the Secretary of the Department of Finance and Administration upon vouchers approved by the Governor or the Department of Health.

Executive Order 2020-004   *Page 4*
State Capitol   •   Room 400   •   Santa Fe, New Mexico 87501   •   505-476-2200   •   fax: 505-476-2226

City at the Crossroads   **199**

11. This Order may be supplemented or amended.

THIS ORDER supersedes any other previous orders, proclamations, or directives in conflict. This Executive Order shall take effect immediately and shall remain in effect until the Governor rescinds it.

ATTEST:

Maggie Toulouse Oliver

MAGGIE TOULOUSE OLIVER
SECRETARY OF STATE

DONE AT THE EXECUTIVE OFFICE
THIS 11TH DAY OF MARCH 2020

WITNESS MY HAND AND THE GREAT
SEAL OF THE STATE OF NEW MEXICO

Michelle Lujan Grisham

MICHELLE LUJAN GRISHAM
GOVERNOR

Executive Order 2020-004   *Page 5*
State Capitol • Room 400 • Santa Fe, New Mexico 87501 • 505-476-2200 • fax: 505-476-2226

200 City at the Crossroads

City of Albuquerque

Office of the Mayor Timothy M. Keller

**DECLARATION OF LOCAL STATE OF EMERGENCY DUE TO NOVEL
CORONAVIRUS COVID-19**

WHEREAS, in December 2019, a novel coronavirus, now designated COVID-19, was detected. Symptoms of COVID-19 include fever, cough, and shortness of breath. Outcomes for those infected with COVID-19 have ranged from mild to severe illness, and in some cases death; and

WHEREAS, on March 11, 2020, the World Health Organization declared that the COVID-19 outbreak should be characterized as a pandemic; and

WHEREAS, on March 11, 2020, New Mexico Governor Michelle Lujan Grisham and the New Mexico Department of Health confirmed the first confirmed cases of COVID-19 in New Mexico; and

WHEREAS, on March 11, 2020, New Mexico Governor Michelle Lujan Grisham issued Executive Order 2020-004, Order Declaring a State of Public Health Emergency and Invoking the Powers Provided by the All Hazard Emergency Management Act and the Emergency Licensing Act; and

WHEREAS, following the issuance of Executive Order 2020-004, there have been additional confirmed cases of COVID-19 in New Mexico, including Bernalillo County and the City of Albuquerque; and

WHEREAS, the identification of "community spread" cases of COVID-19 in the United States signals that the transmission of the virus is no longer strictly limited to travel to high-risk areas, or contact with travelers who have visited high-risk areas; and

WHEREAS, the spread of COVID-19 endangers life and property to such extent that extraordinary measures must be taken to protect the public health, safety, and welfare;

WHEREAS, the City of Albuquerque utilized the local Comprehensive Emergency Management Plan, activated the Emergency Operations Center on several occasions, and performed initial damage assessments relating to COVID-19 that occurred beginning in January 2020;

1

WHEREAS, it is currently impossible for the City of Albuquerque to predict its total eligible uninsured expenditures due to the rapidly evolving nature of this outbreak;

WHEREAS, the City of Albuquerque faces the continuing threat of the spread of COVID-19 and damage caused by COVID-19 until the pandemic subsides and unless the City takes proactive measures to prevent or control the spread of the virus; and

WHEREAS, the emergency expenditures and the overall magnitude of the financial harm due to Executive Order 2020-004 and closing of New Mexico public schools of COVID-19 has yet to be determined; and

WHEREAS, the City of Albuquerque faces the continuing threat of untold damage to public health thereby perpetuating an uncertain financial burden;

WHEREAS, this local emergency constitutes a public health emergency, and the resulting damage is of such magnitude as to be beyond local control and requires the resources of the State to minimize economic and physical harm necessary to protect the public health, safety, and welfare of the people and property in Albuquerque.

NOW, THEREFORE, I, Timothy M. Keller, Mayor of the City of Albuquerque, by virtue of the authority vested in my office by the Laws of the State of New Mexico and the Albuquerque City Code of Ordinances, do hereby Declare a Local State of Emergency to exist throughout the City of Albuquerque due to the disastrous effects from COVID-19 beginning around March 10, 2020. The local state of emergency shall terminate after 48 hours from the issuance thereof, or upon the issuance of a proclamation determining an emergency no longer exists, whichever occurs first. I hereby order that:

1. Pursuant to § 2-9-1-4(C) of the Civil Emergency Powers Ordinance, all places of mass assembly, including but not limited to performance and athletic venues, are to close until the termination of this emergency;

2. Pursuant to § 2-9-1-4(F) of the Civil Emergency Powers Ordinance, all nonessential City-sponsored events and gatherings on or before April 15, 2020, are canceled; and

3. Pursuant to § 2-9-1-4(G) of the Civil Emergency Powers Ordinance, the City may enter any agreements regarding the use of property as necessary to address or mitigate the impact of COVID-19 outside the usual real property requirements of the Revised Ordinances of Albuquerque 1994 ch. 5, art. II, § 5-2-1 *et seq*; and

2

4. Pursuant to § 2-9-1-5 and § 2-9-1-7 of the Civil Emergency Powers Ordinance, the Albuquerque Police Department may enforce this proclamation and all orders contained within and any person who does not comply with this order may be subject to civil penalties; and

5. Pursuant to § 2-9-1-6 of the Civil Emergency Powers Ordinance, the Albuquerque City Council may extend this proclamation for additional periods of time prior to its expiration as it deems necessary; and

6. Pursuant to § 2-9-1-4(H), I may issue other such orders that are imminently necessary for the protection of life and property throughout the duration of this emergency; and

7. Pursuant to §§ 5-5-19(B)(1) and 5-5-35, I find that there are urgent and compelling reasons, including the unforeseen and dangerous situation of the COVID-19 pandemic, enabling the City to make emergency procurements to preserve the peace, health, or safety of people or property within the jurisdiction of the City or to prevent significant economic loss; and

8. I authorize and direct the Chief Administrative Officer to take all actions with respect to City staff as may be necessary to carry out the mission of the city government in emergencies; and

9. The City may issue further proclamations of emergency in response to additional or updated information from the State of New Mexico or the federal government; and

10. As Mayor, I further reserve all other authority and powers conferred by the Revised Ordinances of Albuquerque and New Mexico state law to respond as necessary to this situation.

I REQUEST from the New Mexico State Department of Homeland Security and Emergency Management and other appropriate State agencies, financial assistance to supplement the necessary actions taken in response to the local emergency from COVID-19 that has occurred beginning on March 10, 2020 and culminated in five confirmed cases of COVID-19 on March 13, 2020.

I REQUEST financial assistance from the Federal Emergency Management Agency and other appropriate federal agencies in the event that the President makes future declarations providing funds to local governments to mitigate the costs incurred during this emergency.

This proclamation shall take effect immediately from and after its issuance.

3

SIGNED ON THIS _18_ DAY OF _March_ , 2020.

TIMOTHY M. KELLER
MAYOR OF ALBUQUERQUE

4

INDEX OF NAMES

ABOUT THE AUTHOR

Joline Gutierrez Krueger is a longtime journalist based out of Albuquerque. She worked previously for the *Albuquerque Tribune* and has recently retired from her bi-weekly "UpFront" column she wrote for *The Albuquerque Journal*. Raised in Albuquerque, Gutierrez Krueger lived on both coasts and a few mountain ranges, attended three universities and a number of fellowships and internships, and finally returned home to complete her creative writing degree at the University of New Mexico. *City at the Crossroads* is her first book.

Photo by Donald Glenn

CPSIA information can be obtained
at www.ICGtesting.com
Printed in the USA
BVHW092153140922
647075BV00003B/21